Communications
in Computer and Information Science   2041

Rationale

The CCIS series is devoted to the publication of proceedings of computer science conferences. Its aim is to efficiently disseminate original research results in informatics in printed and electronic form. While the focus is on publication of peer-reviewed full papers presenting mature work, inclusion of reviewed short papers reporting on work in progress is welcome, too. Besides globally relevant meetings with internationally representative program committees guaranteeing a strict peer-reviewing and paper selection process, conferences run by societies or of high regional or national relevance are also considered for publication.

Topics

The topical scope of CCIS spans the entire spectrum of informatics ranging from foundational topics in the theory of computing to information and communications science and technology and a broad variety of interdisciplinary application fields.

Information for Volume Editors and Authors

Publication in CCIS is free of charge. No royalties are paid, however, we offer registered conference participants temporary free access to the online version of the conference proceedings on SpringerLink (http://link.springer.com) by means of an http referrer from the conference website and/or a number of complimentary printed copies, as specified in the official acceptance email of the event.

CCIS proceedings can be published in time for distribution at conferences or as post-proceedings, and delivered in the form of printed books and/or electronically as USBs and/or e-content licenses for accessing proceedings at SpringerLink. Furthermore, CCIS proceedings are included in the CCIS electronic book series hosted in the SpringerLink digital library at http://link.springer.com/bookseries/7899. Conferences publishing in CCIS are allowed to use Online Conference Service (OCS) for managing the whole proceedings lifecycle (from submission and reviewing to preparing for publication) free of charge.

Publication process

The language of publication is exclusively English. Authors publishing in CCIS have to sign the Springer CCIS copyright transfer form, however, they are free to use their material published in CCIS for substantially changed, more elaborate subsequent publications elsewhere. For the preparation of the camera-ready papers/files, authors have to strictly adhere to the Springer CCIS Authors' Instructions and are strongly encouraged to use the CCIS LaTeX style files or templates.

Abstracting/Indexing

CCIS is abstracted/indexed in DBLP, Google Scholar, EI-Compendex, Mathematical Reviews, SCImago, Scopus. CCIS volumes are also submitted for the inclusion in ISI Proceedings.

How to start

To start the evaluation of your proposal for inclusion in the CCIS series, please send an e-mail to ccis@springer.com.

Imen Jemili · Mohamed Mosbah ·
Sabra Mabrouk · Leo Mendiboure

Editors

Distributed Computing for Emerging Smart Networks

4th International Workshop, DiCES-N 2023
Bizerte, Tunisia, May 27, 2023
Revised Selected Papers

 Springer

Editors
Imen Jemili (ID)
University of Carthage
Zarzouna Bizerte, Tunisia

Mohamed Mosbah (ID)
Bordeaux INP
Bordeaux, France

Sabra Mabrouk (ID)
University of Carthage
Zarzouna Bizerte, Tunisia

Leo Mendiboure (ID)
Gustave Eiffel University
Champs-sur-Marne, France

ISSN 1865-0929   ISSN 1865-0937 (electronic)
Communications in Computer and Information Science
ISBN 978-3-031-52822-4   ISBN 978-3-031-52823-1 (eBook)
https://doi.org/10.1007/978-3-031-52823-1

This Springer imprint is published by the registered company Springer Nature Switzerland AG
The registered company address is: Gewerbestrasse 11, 6330 Cham, Switzerland

Paper in this product is recyclable.

Preface

This volume contains the proceedings of the fourth Workshop on Distributed Computing for Emerging Smart Networks (DiCES-N 2023). The workshop was held on May 27, 2023, in Bizerte, Tunisia. We received a total of 13 submissions, of which 6 were accepted for publication, and an invited paper. The acceptance rate was therefore approximately 46,15%. Reviewing was single-blind, where each paper was assigned to at least three reviewers.

The smart city concept has been embraced by several cities around the world, such as Singapore, Zurich, New York, Oslo, London, Nice, and other cities in the European Union; more and more cities are being added to this list. These various smart city initiatives have different objectives, such as achieving an acceptable standard of living for its citizens, raising productivity, and boosting the country's economy or optimizing the use of natural resources. These objectives revolve around smart cities' key applications, mainly smart people, smart governance, smart living, smart economy, smart environment, and smart mobility. In this context, intelligent transport systems (ITS) have benefited from recent advances in different fields and are attracting increasing interest from industry and academia. The first initiatives have started with VANETs[1]. Improving road safety was the main goal of VANETs; this networking paradigm allows communication among vehicles equipped with OBU[2] and roadside units (RSUs) placed along the roads to exchange information about road status, vehicle speed, vehicle position, etc. The advent of the Internet of Things (IoT) and recent technological advances have enabled the proliferation of new applications and innovative services emphasizing entertainment features. These novel advertising services come with diverse demands in terms of throughput, latency, jitter, and so forth; they also bring new QoS[3] and security challenges.

The workshop tackled issues relative to the design, development, and evaluation of distributed systems, platforms, and architectures for Cyber Physical Systems in the context of smart cities. The program included two sessions.

Session 1 was dedicated to Vehicular Networks and emerging technologies. Through the deployment of Intelligent Transport Systems (ITS), the authorities aim to provide efficient solutions to road traffic issues: traffic jams and road accidents due to human errors, mainly speeding, disobeying traffic laws, driving under the influence of alcohol or other substances, or distracted driving. To control road traffic, some fixed sensors can be placed along the road, such as loop detectors or sensors to inspect vehicle speed, or visual traffic surveillance systems can be used to gather high-quality video sequences in real time to detect congestion or identify misbehaviour. Moreover, the constant evolution of the transportation industry has also brought many improvements to modern vehicles in order to ensure road safety and provide a better experience to drivers and passengers;

---

[1] VANETs: Vehicular ad hoc networks.
[2] OBU: On Board Unit.
[3] QoS: Quality of Service.

modern vehicles are now equipped with multiple sensors deployed inside and outside the vehicle to add an extra layer of safety, such as Ultrasonic sensors, RADAR, GPS[4], gyroscopes, accelerometer sensors, and LiDAR sensors; LiDAR technology, being used as an in-vehicle or in-road sensor to detect and measure the distance of objects and generate very high-resolution three-dimensional maps, is introduced in this section. LiDAR technology is a valuable safety mechanism for many vehicular field applications, as it offers an extensive scanning range and accurate identification and classification of objects in the presence or absence of light. Combined with other sensors, a powerful detection system is provided to scan the environment around a moving vehicle and detect obstacles in its path. Indeed, all these different types of sensors gather real-time data about the vehicle's status or its surrounding environment to provide new functionalities and ensure vehicle safety. This huge volume of data being collected in real time thanks to internal or external sensors can now be also exploited to ensure the prediction of the network state in the short and long term by applying emerging technologies, such as machine learning and deep learning. The deployment of such techniques in the smart parking application is discussed in this section. With the improvement of living standards and the steady expansion of urban areas, the number of vehicles continues to grow, leading to congestion and crowding on the streets; it becomes increasingly difficult to find a free parking space, especially during peak hours. Therefore, every driver can waste a huge amount of time driving around the streets or visiting different parking lots to look for a vacant space. Besides, generated traffic jams and road accidents negatively affect urban mobility, the lives of citizens, as well as the economy by blocking access to business districts and large commercial centres or by forcing drivers to park in remote areas, which discourages them from travelling to these destinations. Having an intelligent parking system that can predict free parking spaces is an attractive and efficient solution that could save us this daily time wasted. We can rely on the internet of things, artificial intelligence and/or multi-agent systems to automate the parking process and consider several factors such as the driver's current location, his intended destination, the travel time, the cruising time, and the parking cost to reserve vacant places in parking lots and guide drivers to the selected parking lot. The use of such a smart parking system could significantly improve the driver's experience and help stakeholders to take measures to better manage urban mobility and reduce its negative impacts on modern society and the environment, mainly air pollution from idling vehicles and $CO2$[5] emissions, increased noise, and induced health problems. In fact, nowadays, people are seeking new alternative solutions such as micro-mobility, discussed as the second smart mobility application in this section. Micro-mobility offers a variety of small and lightweight vehicles suitable for trips of less than five miles and more and more persons are using this type of transportation for their daily trip to work or school or for leisure. To cope with this new popular perception, many operators offer rental services for these new transportation modes; their environmental friendliness and ability to relieve traffic congestion and parking demand in urban areas and reduce carbon emissions have promoted the use of shared micro-mobility services such as electric scooters, bikes, and motorcycles. However, this rising new market still faces some challenges related to maintenance difficulties, vandalism diminishing vehicle

---

[4] GPS: Global Positioning System.
[5] CO2: Carbon Dioxide.

life span, infrastructure regulation and safety issues. Fleet maldistribution is also one of the main micro-mobility problems. In fact, each operator provides a specific operating mode for the parking procedure: (i) a dock-based system forcing the user to park at the nearest station to their intended destination or (ii) a free-floating system, which authorizes users to park the fleet freely in the service area. The first mode facilitates the management of micro-vehicles, but it imposes some restrictions on the user. The second mode makes the rental procedure more convenient and easier and offers more freedom to the user; however, it can lead to an unbalanced system since the parking system is not controlled. This fleet maldistribution problem has a negative impact on the operator's revenue and on the quality of the user experience. The unavailability of micro-devices at a given time or in some specific areas causes user dissatisfaction, since he must travel to fetch a micro-vehicle. In this context, micro-mobility operators must implement effective strategies to enhance the services and the overall user experience. To be able to measure, track, and manage fleets remotely, operators generally rely on cellular communications and the information provided through the operator's application. Besides, every device is equipped with a growing array of sensors able to gather real-time data about the device and its environment. This collected data from the shared micro-mobility system, such as trip data, locations, battery status, and traffic data, can be processed and analyzed to optimize fleet placement and reduce maintenance costs, while data provided by the vehicle sensors or traffic data can be useful to identify collision risks and improve user safety.

Session 2 focused on the Safety and Security of intelligent transportation systems. Recent advances associated with autonomous vehicles (AVs) promise to provide comfort and more safety by partially or fully replacing the human driver in the task of driving while avoiding road hazards and adjusting to traffic conditions and traffic signals. To enable such functional behaviour, these vehicles must be equipped with a combination of advanced sensor technology and dotted with on-board and remote processing capabilities. Besides this smartness, they must be totally connected with the rest of the world through a variety of wireless communication technologies. To be operational, such a vehicle must be continuously fed with real-time data about its status, its surroundings, and other relevant information (weather, etc.); this data is processed locally or remotely, raising new security challenges. Indeed, these vehicles, with their interconnected components and heavy reliance on digital infrastructure, create a complex environment potentially sensitive to various types of cyberattacks. For example, hackers may be able to remotely access and infiltrate on-board systems and networks; they may exploit system vulnerabilities. For this reason, it is imperative to identify vulnerabilities and weaknesses early, during the development phase. Proactive detection of potential security flaws will allow developers to implement the necessary countermeasures to mitigate risks before autonomous vehicles are deployed on public roads. Such a critical phase requires comprehensive understanding of the vehicle's architecture, communication protocols, and software systems, as well as the ability to anticipate potential threats and attack vectors. Subsequently, it is necessary to effectively assess and quantify the precise degree of vulnerability of an existing system when exposed to attacks thanks to a variety of methodologies and tools, such as penetration testing, vulnerability scanning, and threat modelling. The first topic, discussed in this section, is related to threat modelling; it exploits UML[6] modelling and a model checker-based approach. It presents a framework which automatically identifies potential threats and generates secure implementation solutions. In addition, a real deployment of connected and autonomous cars underlines the need also to intensify efforts to secure communications between vehicles. Platooning, tackled in this section, is another ITS application relying on self-driving and V2V[7] communication between the different members of the platoon. A platoon is designed primarily for freight transport to allow long-distance trucks to travel together more efficiently; this convoy of vehicles travels in a closely spaced group (platoon) with automated speed and steering control, thereby reducing air drag and improving fuel economy and safety. The platoon leader is responsible for keeping the whole platoon stable by specifying the appropriate speed, the distance between vehicles, and the relevant direction to be followed; this information is communicated to all followers, called members. He also coordinates the various maneuvers like join, leave, split, and dissolve; the joining maneuver, allowing new trucks to be added to the platoon, is one of the most critical operations, as any interference caused by nearby vehicles can delay the successful execution of the maneuver or enable an intruder to be inserted into the platoon, endangering the safety of the whole group. It is imperative to detect these intrusions promptly and to take the appropriate measures.

The last topic focused on accidents at level crossings (LC), which have attracted considerable attention in recent years and cause dramatic material and human damage. Indeed, an LC is an intersection where a railway line intersects with a road or path at the same level. Most accidents occur at passive level crossings. Indeed, active warning devices are effective in avoiding accidents due to road user errors, such as inattention, or insufficient visibility. In this context, ITS can rely on new technologies, affordable now, to enhance road safety and reduce the risk of accidents. Equipping passive level crossings with appropriate sensors that can detect the arrival of trains and with warning devices would increase safety; Vehicle-to-Everything (V2X) communications can be exploited to give rail and road users real-time traffic information and to ensure alert dissemination when dangerous circumstances are identified. For such complex and critical systems, it is imperative to ensure that they behave correctly in all possible situations to guarantee their safety and the users' safety. Formal methods can be of great help for the designer to evaluate the behaviour of a system and avoid errors before its implementation.

We are grateful for the support provided by the many people who contributed to the success of DiCES-N 2023. Naturally, the workshop could not take place without the efforts made by the Organizing Committee who helped us to organize and publicize the event, particularly the Technical Program Committee (Sabra Mabrouk and Leo Mendiboure), the local organizers (Emna Ben Salem and Soumaya Dahi) and the publicity chair (Zeineb El Khalfi).

We are also thankful to the members of the Program Committee for providing their valuable time and helping us to review the received papers. We would also like to thank the authors for submitting and then revising a set of high-quality papers. Finally, we

---

[6] UML: Unified Modeling Language.
[7] V2V: Vehicle to Vehicle.

express our sincere gratitude to Springer for giving us the opportunity to publish in CCIS and we appreciate the support and advice provided by the editorial team.

May 2023

Imen Jemili
Mohamed Mosbah
Sabra Mabrouk
Leo Mendiboure

Organization

General Chairs

Imen Jemili   University of Carthage, Tunisia
Mohamed Mosbah   Bordeaux INP, France

Program Committee Chairs

Sabra Mabrouk   University of Carthage, Tunisia
Leo Mendiboure   Gustave Eiffel University, France

Local Organization

Emna Ben Salem   University of Carthage, Tunisia
Soumaya Dahi   University of Carthage, Tunisia

Publicity Chair

Zeineb El Khalfi   CESI, France

Program Committee

Salma Batti   University of Carthage, Tunisia
Raoudha Beltaifa   University of Manouba, Tunisia
Anis Ben Aicha   University of Carthage, Tunisia
Lotfi Ben Othmane   Iowa State University, USA
Ismail Berrada   Mohammed VI Polytechnic University, Morocco
Afaf Bouhoute   Sidi Mohamed Ben Abdellah University, Morocco
Luca Davoli   University of Parma, Italy
Kamal E Melkemi   University of Batna 2, Algeria
Ahmed EL Oualkadi   National School of Applied Sciences of Tangier, Morocco
Secil Ercan   Gustave Eiffel University, France
Tahani Gazdar   University of Jeddah, Saudi Arabia

Contents

Contents

Vehicular Networks and Emerging Technologies

Survey on Lidar Sensing Technology for Vehicular Networks

Mouaouia Guinoubi$^{(\boxtimes)}$

University of Carthage, Tunis, Tunisia
mouawiya93@gmail.com

Abstract. Object detection systems are the principal pillar in various safety applications in the transportation field; various sensors can be deployed to detect and track moving objects and obstacles. In this context, LiDAR technology has shown its effectiveness. In this work, we survey LiDAR technology focusing on its functioning, sensor types and application fields. In particular, we point out its use in the vehicular field and outline the different steps followed by LiDAR-based object detection approaches.

Keywords: LiDAR · Vehicular networks · Feature extraction · Object detection

1 Introduction

The transportation industry is constantly evolving to improve the driver and passenger experience and road safety. Modern vehicles are equipped with innovative features such as route guidance systems (e.g., automatic emergency braking, adaptive cruise control, lane departure warning, speed assistance monitoring, etc.), fatigue detection [1], voice control, etc. Along with population growth, these enhancements have increased the demand for vehicles, resulting in road congestion and higher accident rates. According to the World Health Organization [2], about 1.3 million people die each year because of road accidents caused by human errors, including speeding, disobeying traffic laws, driving under alcohol or other substances, or distracted driving.

To lower the high rate of accidents, scientists needed to find a method to reduce the risk of human errors while driving; for this reason, multiple sensors can be deployed inside and outside the vehicle to add an extra layer of safety. Some essential sensors are placed on the engine to inform the driver of the state of brakes, engine temperate, engine oil level, etc. Nowadays, there are new 2D and 3D sensing technologies deployed inside the car that enable the drivers to adjust different equipments of the vehicle without looking away from the road using simple hand gestures. For example, a touch screen that is used to adjust the air conditioner and the side windows, a camera installed on the steering wheel that detects specific gestures of the driver in order to answer phone calls or skip songs. In addition, a camera attached to the reverse mirror monitors the driver's state and sees any signs of tiredness on his face. Concerning the sensors

I. Jemili et al. (Eds.): DiCES-N 2023, CCIS 2041, pp. 3–27, 2024.
https://doi.org/10.1007/978-3-031-52823-1_1

used outside the car, in 2000, Nissan's Infiniti luxury division added cameras in the rear of the vehicles that broadcast live video to the drivers to help them view the area behind the car while reversing [3]. In 2003, Toyota launched the Intelligent Parking Assist option in cars by installing ICS[1] sensors on the front and rear bumpers of the vehicle to parallel driverless parking [4]. In 2014, Elon Musk was the first to introduce the self-driving car with the Model S, using many sensors all around the car, from short-range to long-range cameras to Radars and ultrasonic sensors. In 2020, Waymo manufactured a self-driving taxi for public use and it implemented the LiDAR Technology as primary sensing method [5]. These new services are allowed thanks to embedded sensors such as GPS[2] sensors, ultrasonic sensors, cameras, motion sensors, etc.

This work focuses on a new type of sensing technology used for object detection methods known as LiDAR (LiDAR: Light Detection and Ranging). It uses laser beams to generate three-dimensional maps of the vehicle's surrounding environment. It has been adopted as a reliable sensing technology by multiple companies like Waymo, Tesla, and Cruise. LiDAR sensing technology is becoming a more and more stable and reliable method for mainly autonomous vehicles. Many surveys have introduced LiDAR technology [6–8]. Other surveys like [6] and [7] focused on the sensing mechanism of the LiDAR sensor and the way it functions, while [8] gave a detailed taxonomy to the 3D object detection methods that are based on LiDAR sensing data. In this survey, we will focus on the use of LiDAR technology, mainly in the vehicular field.

In this paper, we presented a survey of a LiDAR sensing technology. We included a general introduction to the LiDAR sensing system and its different fields of application while focusing on the vehicular field. In addition, we gave a brief comparison between this technology and other sensing technologies and presented its main advantages and disadvantages. Finally, we presented the different step of object detection process using this LiDAR technology and its different methods of application.

The rest of the paper is organized as follows. In Sect. 2, we briefly introduce the LiDAR technology, explaining its operating mode and range of applications. Section 3 focuses on LiDAR technology in the vehicular field. In Sect. 4, we conclude our paper.

2   LiDAR Technology

In the context of smart mobility, different types of sensors can be deployed to provide new functionalities and in particular to ensure vehicle safety, as mentioned in [9]; the authors classified employed sensors into two categories: (i) in-vehicle sensors including Ultrasonic sensors, RADAR, GPS, Gyro-scope, accelerometer sensors, and LiDAR sensor; (ii) and in-road sensors such as pneumatic road tube, inductive loop detector, magnetic sensors, piezoelectric, infra-red sensor, acoustic array sensors, radio-frequency identification, and LiDAR sensor. Each sensing technology has its advantages and disadvantages; in Table 1, we summarize the most used ones.

---

[1] ICS: Intelligent Clearance Sonar.
[2] GPS:Global Positioning System.

Table 1. Sensing technologies.

Sensor	Advantages	Disadvantages	Applications
RGB cameras	– Provide dense pixel image – Low price with decent data	– Provide no information concerning the depth of objects – Sensitive in poorly lit, and highly occluded environments and bad weather	**In-vehicle sensors:** – Monitor the surroundings of the vehicle and broadcast it to the driver – Monitor the driver health state (fatigue) for emergency alerts – Detect the face of a person in the case of a stolen car – Autonomous driving **In-Road sensors:** – Monitor the traffic – Detect violations of road code – Detect researched cars
Stereo cameras	– Provide dense pixel image – Provide depth information for objects – Low price compared to LiDAR with decent data	– Sensitive in bad weather conditions, poorly lit and highly occluded environments – More expensive than RGB cameras – Depth error increases exponentially based on the distance – Provide data that demand more computational power	**In-vehicle sensors:** – Obstacle detection – Road surface scanning **In-Road sensors:** – Application to inspect the state of the road
RADAR	– Low price – Wireless technology – Capable of detecting the speed of an object – Wide range field of view – Able to collect data in harsh weather conditions – The single can go through insulators	– Low-resolution depth maps – short-range field of view – Can't provide the color of the object – Sensitive to radio frequencies – Fail to differentiate between multiple objects	**In-vehicle sensors:** – Used for collision avoidance – Safety applications (occupant detection) **In-Road sensors:** – Speed measurement – Detection of the direction of movement of the vehicle
Ultrasonic sensors	– Low price – Not affected by luminosity	– Low-resolution depth maps – A small field of view – Mediocre accuracy (unable to differentiate between small and big objects) – Can be affected by loud noises	**In-vehicle sensors:** – Parking applications – Warning applications – Autonomous driving – Used for traffic congestion detection **In-Road sensors:** – Traffic measurement – Vehicle detection – Highway Vehicle Violation Detection
LiDAR	– Not affected by the lighting condition of the environment – Accurate, quick, and High resolution depth maps over long distances (longer than the Radar and stereo cameras)	– High cost for high-end sensors – Low resolution for low-end sensors – Occlusion problem – Sensitive in foggy weather – The data generated is usually sparse and take time to process – Can't provide information about the texture of the objects	**In-vehicle sensors:** – Parking applications – Warning applications – Autonomous driving – Used for traffic congestion detection – Monitor the state of the railroad **In-Road sensors:** – Traffic measurement – Vehicle detection – Train arrival detection – Autonomous driving

As shown in Table 1, several sensors could be deployed to ensure the safety of the roads, for example, RGB cameras can be placed on the roadsides to detect vehicles, congested points of traffic, and even license plates of cars in case of road violation. RADAR sensors can be used to detect the speed of moving vehicles, while ultrasonic sensors are wildly used for parking assistant systems. In addition to the services mentioned above, these sensors can also be combined into a detection system to scan the environment around a moving vehicle and detect obstacles in its path. In this work, we will focus on LiDAR technology, as it provides high spatial resolutions range information, useful for many road safety applications such as ADAS (Advanced Driver Assistance Systems) [10], inspecting of railroad infrastructure [11,12], and inspecting the road pavement condition [13].

In this section, we first explain how LiDAR technology works, then we enumerate the different types of LiDAR sensors and their respective fields of application.

2.1 LiDAR Scanning

a. LiDAR System Components: LiDAR is part of the Optical Wireless communication (OCW) technologies used to generate very high-resolution three-dimensional maps. The LiDAR technology is considered an active remote sensing system because it generates beams of light (ultraviolet, visible, or near-infrared) to detect and measure the distance of objects and generate very high-resolution three-dimensional maps called point clouds. Every LiDAR system is composed of three essential elements:

■ **The LiDAR sensor:** These pieces of equipment come in different shapes and sizes, but most of them have a general component structure, as illustrated in Fig. 1:

- *The Transmitter:* it represents the light source (e.g., laser, LED[3], or VCSL[4] diode) that generates and emits, in pulses, laser beams from the sensor to the objects.
- *Scanner and optics:* a combination of plane mirrors, a polygon mirror, and a dual-axis scanner are used to adjust the angle and range of the detected laser beams.
- *Photodetector:* also known as receiver electronics or photodiode, is the light sensor responsible for collecting the laser beams reflected off the objects and converting them into an electrical signal. There are two principal photodetector technologies used in LiDAR: solid-state electronics (e.g., photodiodes) and Photomultiplier.

---

[3] LED:Light Emitting Diode.
[4] VCSL: Vertical Cavity Surface-emitting Laser.

■ **Position and navigation systems:** it includes a GPS receiver and IMU[5], usually needed when the sensor is attached to a moving platform (car, airplanes, satellites, etc.) to identify the location and orientation of the LiDAR sensor in the X, Y, Z space, alongside the characteristics of the objects like the distance, size, and shape.

■ **A computer and software:** they are used to correlate all the information from the LiDAR sensor and the navigation system and generate the point clouds.

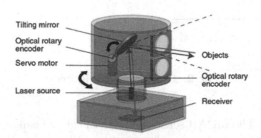

Fig. 1. General representation of a LiDAR sensor [6]

b. LiDAR Functioning: The LiDAR technology is like RADAR because both sensors generate and send out multiple waves of energy that travel from the Transmitter to the objects around them. Then, based on the time-of-flight principle as exposed in Fig. 2, they measure the distance separating them from the things; the used equation is:

$$D = c * \frac{t}{2} \tag{1}$$

where:

t: represents the time of flight
c: is the constant value of the speed of light

The main difference between both technologies is that RADAR uses radio waves while LiDAR uses light waves. Part of this transmitted signal is reflected from the objects and collected by the receiver component of the LiDAR sensor. This reflected energy, known as the Intensity, is collected by the receiver component of the LiDAR sensor and processed by the Global Positioning System and the Internal Measurement Unit to determine calculate multiple objectives like the location and orientation of the LiDAR sensor in the X, Y, Z space, alongside the characteristics of the objects surrounding it like the distance, size, and shape.

---

[5] IMU: Inertial Measurement Unit.

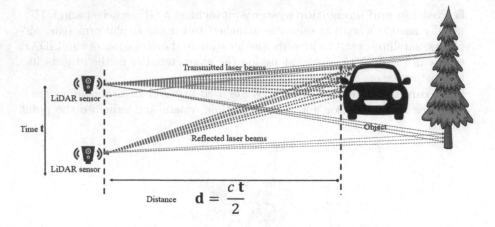

Fig. 2. Time-of-flight principle

c. LiDAR Data: The LiDAR sensor collects the laser beams reflected from the objects, then processes and stores them in files called point clouds that contain information on a significant number of 3D elevation points in a matrix form.

The main four characteristics of each LiDAR point are the three-dimensional coordinates x, y, and z and the Intensity value that represents the strength of the returned laser pulse in addition to other optional pieces of information that are generated by specific sensors:

- Point classification: each point will be given a class that defines the object it is reflected. American Society for Photogrammetry and Remote Sensing (ASPRS) defines these classifications. For example, as shown in Table 2, a point cloud is given one of the twenty classes.
- RGB: some sensors can assign a color to each point of the points cloud based on the intensity of the returned laser beams (points with higher Intensity have warmer tone colors).
- GPS time: this attribute is usually assigned when using a mobile LiDAR sensor (e.g., attached to a moving vehicle) to stamp when the laser beam was emitted from the sensor.

The generated point clouds are stored in files under hundreds of file formats, depending on the LiDAR sensor deployed to scan the area. Still, the majority fall under the ASCII[6] and Binary format.

The first type uses text to encode information, making it easier to read by text editors and other applications (e.g., Microsoft Excel) and optimal for long-term archiving. However, these files take longer to process and to read line by line and are more significant than binary files. This format's most used file types are XYZ, OBJ, PTX, and ASC. The latter format is more compact and can

---

[6] ASCII: American Standard Code for Information Interchange.

Table 2. Classification value and meaning for LiDAR points [?]

Classification value	Meaning
0	Never classified
1	Unassigned
2	Ground
3	Low Vegetation
4	Medium Vegetation
5	High Vegetation
6	Building
7	Low Point
8	Reserved
9	Water
10	Rail
11	Road Surface
12	Reserved
13	Wire - Guard (Shield)
14	Wire - Conductor (Phase)
15	Transmission Tower
16	Wire-Structure Connector (Insulator)
17	Bridge Deck
18	High Noise
19–63	Reserved
64–255	User Definable

store and transmit more information than the ASCII format; it allows faster processing and viewing of files. Its main drawback is that simple text editors cannot read it. FLS, PCD[7] and LAS, are some of the most popular point cloud binary formats.

Other files can store ASCII and binary forms like PLY, FBX, and E57, taking advantage of both formats. However, since both of these formats have their properties, it is not advised to convert binary format to ASCII because it could degrade the value of information.

There is a wide variety of software capable of processing LiDAR point clouds, depending on the format of the files. Open-source software provides a limited number of services; mainly they are used to visualize and display point clouds (e.g., QCIS3 [14], Whitebox GAT [15], Fugro Viewer [16], SAGA GIS [17], GRASS GIS [18], Meshlab [19], CloudCompare [20], etc.). Desktop software offers more services and options in addition to the free viewing mode (e.g., Faro Scene [21], Leica Cyclone [22], Trimble Real works [23], Bentley Pointools [24],

---

[7] PCD: Point Cloud Data.

PointCab [25], Point Fuse [26], EdgeWise [27], Capturing Reality [28], Autodesk ReCap [29], etc.). Table 3 exposes examples of point cloud software and the file formats they can import and export.

Table 3. Point cloud Softwares import and export format

Software	Bentley Pointools	Capturing Reality	Leica Cyclone	Faro Scene	Trimble Real works	Autodesk ReCap
Import format	POD, OBJ, SHP, DXF, DWG, ESRI, E57, ZFS, LAZ, LAS, FLS, FWS, XYZ, PTS, PTX, PTZ, TXT, LWO	PTX, E57	XYZ, PTS, PTX, LAS, E57, ZFS, DP	XYZ, CVS, COR	XYZ, E57, LAS, LAZ, ZFS, RSP, FLS, DP, PTX, PTS	ASC, CL3, CLR, E57, FLS, FWS, ISPROJ, LAS, PCG, PTG, PTS, PTX, RDS, TXT, XYB, XYZ, ZFS, ZFPRJ, DXF, DWG
Export format	POD, PTS, XYZ	OBJ, PLY, XYZ, DSM	XYZ, PTS, PTX, E57, DXF, PCI/CWF, DBX, Land XML	PTC, PTX, PST, XYZ, DXF, IGES, VRML, E57	E57, ASC, LAS 1.2, LAS 1.4, LAZ, POD, PTS, PTX, TZF, BSF	RCS, RCP, PCG, PTS, E57, DXF, DWG

Although the LiDAR data is relatively new, it is available for researchers and scientists to download and experiment with through different websites like Open Topography [30], USGS Earth Explorer [31], NOAA Digital Coast [32], and National Ecological Observatory Network [33]. These websites provide a fixed-point view of LiDAR data irrelevant in the case of model training and machine learning. In addition, different companies offer free datasets for scientists to apply and create new machine learning models like Waymo [5], Kitti dataset [34], and Ouster which alongside its data, it provides unique software used to display and manipulate the information.

2.2 LiDAR Types

Generally, there are two different types of LiDAR application, airborne and terrestrial. Each type requires LiDAR sensors with specific characteristics related to the application objective, the diameter of the area to be scanned, the maximum range of the laser beam needed, and the cost of the sensor.

a. Airborne LiDAR: The airborne LiDAR is an acquisition method that involves attaching the LiDAR sensor to a flying airplane, a helicopter, or a drone to create a top viewpoint cloud over large areas, as shown in Fig. 3.

This system comprises three main elements:

- The LiDAR scanner
- A GPS device that detects the position of the aircraft holding the scanner
- The IMU is responsible for processing the LiDAR data, generating the point cloud, and recording the airplane's altitude.

Fig. 3. Example of airborne LiDAR scanning method [35]

The aircraft's height affects the accuracy and density of the point clouds generated by this method. The longer the distance between the airplane and the ground, the lower quality of the data. Compared with the traditional methods, using high-quality RGB cameras to capture top view images, it is possible to filter the vegetation from the point clouds captured by the airborne LiDAR sensors, leaving only the relevant ground surfaces, as shown in Fig. 4.

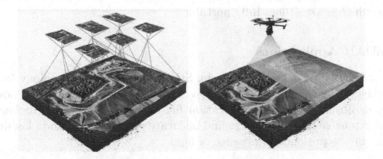

Fig. 4. Comparison between LiDAR sensing and photogrammetry [36]

The sensors used for these situations are divided into topographic and Bathymetric sensors. Both sensors operate under the same concept, but the main difference is the LiDAR scanners' capabilities. Topographic scanners used to be mounted on airplanes because of their significant sizes (e.g., Leica TerrainMapper-2, Leica SPL100, RIEGL VQ-880-G, Galaxy T2000, ALTM Galaxy, Trimble AX60i, Trimble AX80), but more companies started manufacturing more compacted sensors that produce inferior but acceptable results. Hence, attaching them to small drones (e.g., DJI M600 Pro LiDAR quadcopter, Draganflyer Commander, Riegl RiCopter Lidar UAV) became possible. This method generates a colored point cloud for above-land surfaces like railroads, highways, and infrastructures while avoiding the potential terrestrial obstacles that could slow down the process or affect the final result of the captured point cloud. Bathymetric LiDAR sensors are physically more significant, more powerful, and require a vital energy source to function. They are usually mounted on airplanes and used to measure the depth of lakes, seas, and oceans or to locate objects underwater and map out the structure of the land under sea level.

b. Terrestrial LiDAR: Terrestrial LiDAR sensors are installed at the ground level and classified into Mobile and Static sensors. With the mobile LiDAR, it is possible to use more than one laser scanner mounted on a moving vehicle (e.g., cars, trains, boats, and vans) to generate dense point clouds along the vehicle's trajectory. Similar to the airborne LiDAR, mobile sensors (e.g., Topcon IP-S3, Ultra Puck, Alpha Prime, HDL-32E, MRS1000, MRS6000, Valeo Scala, Ouster OS0, OS1, OS2, ES2) are usually equipped with a GPS to detect the location of the vehicle, and an IMU to process the data coming from the LiDAR sensor and the navigation system.

Static sensors, also known as stationary terrestrial sensors (e.g., Faro Focus 3Dx130, Leica C10, Riegl VZ series, Topcon GLS 1500), are commonly used for surveying purposes. They are placed on a fixated tripod at a strategic location to create three-dimensional maps of a specific region from a particular angle. Compared to the traditional methods, static LiDAR sensors can scan in every direction, including upwards and they can easily be relocated after completing one scan which makes them fully portable.

2.3 LiDAR Applications

LiDAR was first introduced by Malcolm Stitch in 1961 as a technology for satellite tracking. This technology has evolved over the years, and it is now successfully deployed in various application fields that require a technology that offers an extensive scanning range and accurate identification and classification of objects in the presence or absence of light:

- Agriculture: The agriculture sector is one of the oldest and longest-existing markets; it always benefits from new technologies. LiDAR technology is very useful in this field; it is possible to attach sensors to drones and capture bird's eye view maps that are later processed to study the soil and the terrain. Based on the height level of crops, it is possible to determine the areas with low productivity that need fertilizers, and damaged crops and products, which will help the farmer avoid potential financial loss.
- Archaeology: The LiDAR technology has been deployed in the archaeology field because it's a low-cost method that can generate high-resolution 3-dimensional maps of archaeological features like ancient caves, roads, fences, terraces, and even boundaries hidden by vegetation without damaging them. In 2009, the archaeologist Chris Fisher discovered a great city of the Purepecha empire that goes back to 1519 [37]; Fisher stated that with

traditional radar technology, it took them two years to survey only 2 km of the site, but with the LiDAR technology it took them only 45 min to scan the entire 13 km surface.

- Forestry: In the forestry field, airborne LiDAR technology has been deployed to study leaf areas, biomass measurements, and canopy heights and estimate the biodiversity of plants, animals, and even fungi. For example, in 2020, LiDAR sensors were used to map the Australian forests that have been damaged by fire and identify the healthy and burned vegetation. Also, the Save the Redwoods League organization [38] has used LiDAR technology to evaluate the height of trees and learn about the biodiversity of redwood forests.
- Geology: The point clouds generated by airborne and terrestrial LiDAR have been used in the geology field to study the surface of the Earth. Such as river channel banks and terraces, glacial landforms, the texture of the terrains under the vegetation level, and observing the elevation changes of landscapes between scanning over a long period. For example, in 2005, the Mont Blanc massif was the first high alpine mountain to be scanned by LiDAR to detect rock falls caused by climate changes [39]. In addition, ts technology was combined with GNSS[8] to locate the Seattle Fault in Washington [40].
- Atmosphere: There are several applications of LiDAR to the atmosphere. Studying the atmosphere using laser beams goes back to before the Second World War in 1930 by Edward Hutchinson Synge, who suggested examining the upper atmosphere using laser beams. Either terrestrial or airborne LiDAR could be deployed for atmospheric applications. For example, cloud classification uses a powerful laser to retrieve cloud tops, aerosol properties investigated by the EARLINET[9] [41], atmospheric gazes measuring (e.g., ozone, water vapor), and atmospheric temperature measuring approximately 120 m above ground.
- Law enforcement: LiDAR technology is being used as a speed gun by the police to detect the speed of vehicles surpassing the speed limit or as a method that records crime scenes to help with the investigation.
- Military: The most general application of the LiDAR system in the military sector is developing a counter-land mine method by the Areté Associates [42] called ALMDS[10] [43].
- Mining: The LiDAR technology has been applied in the mining field by attaching sensors on robots that are wirelessly controlled to map the inside of tunnels and create three-dimensional point clouds [44]. In general, the airborne LiDAR method is the most used for the surveillance of mining sites because of its flexibility against obstacles, and the small size of drones makes them able to reach small spaces [45].
- Physics and astronomy: The Lunar Orbiter Laser Altimeter (LOLA) is a Moon orbiting satellite equipped with a powerful LiDAR that measures the distance between the Earth and the moon's surface in millimeters, and generating topographic maps. Similar to the previous example, the Mars Orbiting

---

[8] GNSS: Gobal Navigation Satellite System.
[9] EARLINET: European Aerosol Research Lidar Network.
[10] ALMDS: Airborne Laser Mine Detection System.

Laser Altimeter (MOLA) is a Mars-orbiting satellite equipped with a powerful LiDAR sensor to generate global surveys of the red planet.
- Rbobotics: LiDAR technology has been embedded in robots; through the generated three-dimensional maps of the environment, it is possible for robots to precisely detect and calculate the distance of the objects around them and classify them using machine learning models.

The latest advancement to the LiDAR technology, as of the time this paper was published, are the development of solid-state LiDAR sensors that uses no moving parts which makes it smaller, more reliable and less expensive. In addition, the recent advancement to this technology is called the multi-spectral LiDAR, which uses multiple wavelengths of light to identify more information about the environment such as the materials of the objects. Finally, this technology is being integrated in different mobile devices like smartphones and tablets, which allow it to be applied in a wider range of applications (e.g. indoor mapping, augmented reality).

Some of the main applications that utilize LiDAR are exposed in Fig. 5 with their respective LiDAR sensors.

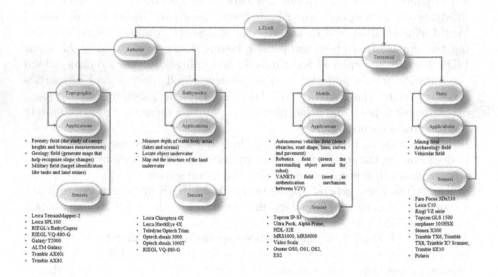

Fig. 5. LiDAR technology classification, applications, and sensor examples.

In this paper, we will explore the use of LiDAR on the field of autonomous driving and the object detection systems when using terrestrial LiDAR sensors.

3   LiDAR Usage in the Vehicular Field

The LiDAR technology is a valuable safety mechanism for other vehicular field applications:

- It was used in the railroad field to improve safety by installing a terrestrial LiDAR at a level crossing point to detect the obstacles and then alert the train driver [46].
- Monitor the state of the railway tracks by attaching a LiDAR sensor on the front of the train to detect irregularities [47–49] that need to be fixed to avoid future accidents.
- Detect objects on the tracks using the airborne LiDAR sensor method [50,51].
- Predict rockfall hazard near railway furthermore.
- Used in the domain of VANets as a solution to ensure secure authentication between vehicles [52].

Still, the autonomous vehicle field remains the field that utilizes LiDAR technology the most as an object detection mechanism [8,53]. In addition, since early 2010, there have been a decent number of research papers that focus on enhancing the perception of vehicles. We will explore the object detection by the LiDAR technology in the vehicular field.

3.1 LiDAR-Based Object Detection in the Vehicular Field

In the vehicular domain, object detection approaches rely either on raw LiDAR data or on the data provided by LiDAR and a camera; indeed, the fusion of LiDAR technology and RGB cameras offered a stable and feasible solution. The raw data coming from either the LiDAR sensor or the RGB camera must go through three phases:

1. The first phase is the data representation, which is responsible for processing, organizing, and structuring the raw data from the LiDAR sensor for the next step.
2. The second phase is feature extraction which is responsible for generating feature maps by extracting different types of features.
3. The third step is the object detection model. Different approaches can be applied in this step: regression of bounding boxes, determining the object orientation, object class prediction, and deduction of object speed in some cases.
4. The last phase is adopted by models that rely on a two-stage architecture. The first phase is the primary object detection step, which is responsible for extracting the bounding boxes framing the detected objects. Afterward, a second step, called Prediction Refinement, is applied to fine-tune and improve the results of the first stage.

As illustrated in Fig. 6, the authors in [8] sum up the different methods of each step of the 3D object detection process.

a. Data Representations: This represents the first step in any 3D object detection process. The raw LiDAR point data is refined to enhance the performance of the next phase of the process which is the feature extraction. As illustrated in Fig. 7, this step includes different methods with different output formats for the LiDAR point clouds data, these methods are explained next.

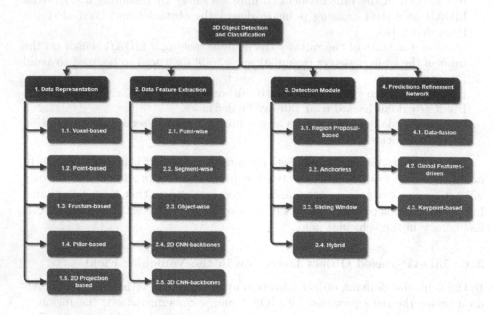

Fig. 6. 3D object detection system steps and their respective methods

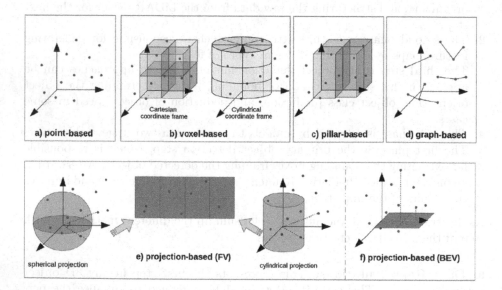

Fig. 7. Feature extraction output formats [53].

- **Point-based:** The concept of this first approach is simple to apply; the form of the point cloud is preserved as a collection of sparse points, then each point is represented by its feature vector generated by combining the features of their neighboring points. But since it is composed of thousands of points, object detection could take a significant amount of time to process. For this reason, a preprocessing step is required in order to compact the size of the point cloud to a pre-defined value [54–59]. The reduction of the point cloud size is made by a procedure known as downsampling, which eliminates points from the point cloud until reaching the required number of points N (N is the fixed number of points in a point cloud). The downsampling can be applied in two ways, either through a random selection method or a Furthest Point Sampling (FPS)algorithm. In the first method, the points are picked randomly until reaching N-selected points, which could result in an uneven selection of points since dense regions of the point cloud have a higher probability of being downsampled than sparse ones [54,55]. The second method starts by picking a point randomly, calculating all the distances of other points, and then deleting the farthest one. This process is repeated until reaching the desired prefixed number of points N; this approach maintains a similar representation to the initial point cloud but at the cost of time and hardware [59–61].
- **Voxel-based:** Voxelization is assigning each point of the point cloud to a voxel according to its 3D coordinates. A voxel is a cubic shape element with distinct coordinates in the 3D space. This approach divides the point clouds into three-dimensional cuboid [62] that could be uniformly spaced or have different sizes inside the x, y, and z Cartesian coordinate grid. In the following step, the features of the raw point cloud are deducted from the group of points inside each voxel as a single feature vector instead of extracting them from each point separately, which lower the computational cost and reduce memory consumption. Some of the features that could be deducted from each voxel are (i) the average value of the intensities inside the voxel, (ii) the 3D coordinates of each voxel point, (iii) and the mean distance between each point and the center of its voxel.
- **Pillar-based:** This method was introduced by [63]; it is based on partitioning the point cloud along the Z-axis (in vertical columns) and splitting the 3D space into fixed-size pillars, which are usually viewed as an unbound voxel along the Z-axis. Like the voxel-based approach, the allocation of points to the pillars is done through Fixed or Dynamic voxelization.
- **Frustum-based:** The models using this data representation [64–66] cut the point clouds into frustums, which is a section that lies between two parallel planes of a cone or a pyramid shape, then apply feature extraction methods on these sections.
- **2D Projection-based:** This data representation method involves projecting three-dimensional point clouds into two-dimensional ones to reduce the computational cost of processing the data. In the literature, three main projection approaches are proposed and applied in various research projects, which are the Range View (RV), the Bird's Eye View (BEV), and Front View (FV).

– **Graph-based:** This last approach converts the point cloud into a graph, where each point is considered a node, and each link between it and its neighbors is an edge. However, since the point cloud holds thousands of points, the number of edges connecting points will be considerably high, resulting in a high computational time and resources. Therefore, this method is preceded by a voxelization step followed by a downsampling phase to preserve specific points [67].

Features Extraction from LiDAR Data: Features extraction is the fundamental phase before applying an object detection method. It enhances the system's performance by providing well-defined and easy-to-process features from the point cloud. There are mainly three classes of features that could be extracted:

– **Local:** also known as low-level features, they represent the spatial information of each point in the point cloud. They are usually extracted at the start of the model pipeline.
– **Global:** also named high-level features, they encapsulate the information of the shape and geometric features between a point and its neighbors; they could be extracted from a single network or through a combination of networks.
– **Contextual:** these features are the last to be extracted and fed to the model object detection phase. They represent the combination between the localization features of points and their semantic value.

Many research methods rely on combining multiple feature extractors to optimize the results of the detection model. There are two different groups of feature extractors, 3D-based and 2D-based extractors. The earlier extractor is applied directly to the 3D space, while the latter operates in the 2D planes; each type has its distinct architectures and application methods.

Object Detection: Object detection is the principal phase of the 3D object detection process; detection approaches can be classified into five categories based on (1) the feature extraction pattern, (2) the pipeline architecture of the detected module, (3) the detection settings of the approach, (4) the object detection mechanisms, and (5) the type of data used as input, as illustrated in Fig. 8. This section will present these classifications.

1. Feature extraction patterns: The phase of the feature extraction process differs from one approach to another. For example, some merge multiple feature extractors to exploit the advantages of different methods, while others use a single method that enhances the execution time of the feature extraction phase. In addition, the architecture of the feature extractor varies from one to another to extract rich information while maintaining spatial information to enhance classification and object localization. When working with a

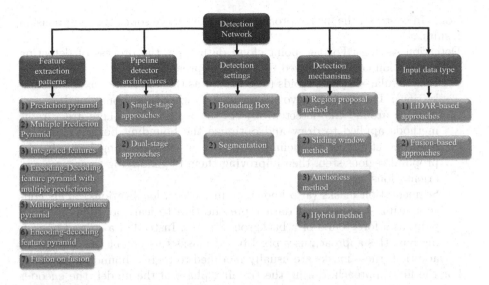

Fig. 8. Different classifications of Detection Networks

three-dimensional type of data, the size and shape of objects are constantly changing depending on the distance between the targeted object and the sensor and the angle of detection; it is necessary to implement networks capable of extracting multi-scale features. Approaches like [68,69] that operate on 2D images attempted to achieve this objective by performing object detection while resizing the input images; but, come with a high computational cost. More recent approaches [70] tried another method by increasing the layers of the decoders in the encoder/decoder architecture, which led to generating feature vectors with multiple resolutions.

2. Pipeline Detector architecture: The object detection solutions generally follow two different architectures:
   - The dual-stage approaches: the detection approaches that follow this architecture are composed of two networks. The first starts with a proposal generator (e.g., RPN) to create a set of region predictions known as Intermediate proposals. Then, a second network known as the Prediction Refinement Network is used to optimize the localization accuracy of the detected objects that takes as inputs the generated proposals and the original point coordinates features.
   - The Single-Stage approaches: these approaches combine the classification and bounding box proposals into a collection of connected layers. They directly apply object classification and generate final bounding box estimations for each part of the feature maps without the need to use the bounding box refinement phase.

Compared with the dual-stage approach, the single-stage is usually more time-efficient, making it more suitable for real-time object detection applications. In contrast, the first approach can achieve more sophisticated precision results.

3. Detection settings: For the point cloud data type, the process of detecting object location can be achieved using two approaches:

   - Rectangular-shaped cuboids (also known as the bounding box level localization): This concept revolves around drawing tight bounding box predictions around the detected objects to locate them. There are various methods applied to draw and optimize the bounding boxes. The most used one starts by pre-defining the size of the bounding boxes in the proposal regions step, then improving them by modifying their sizes and orientations.

   - Segmentation masks (also known as mask-level localizations): This concept utilizes point-based data representation to learn and classify each point as a foreground or a background point. Instead of a cuboid bounding box, this approach uses pixel-based masks to segment the objects. In addition, these masks are usually modified to regress bounding boxes.

   For the first approach, during the training phase of the model, the encoder networks utilize the feature vectors generated by the feature extraction phase and the annotation files that store the dimensions of the bounding boxes. The training step of the second phase uses the point-based features extracted from the ground truth segmentation masks provided by the datasets. Finally, the IoU mechanism is used between the bounding boxes generated by the model and the ground truth provided by the dataset to evaluate the detector's performance.

4. Detection Mechanisms: The object detection approaches can be divided into four main techniques based on the methods used to generate the region proposals, and they are described in the following:

   - Region proposal method Several examples and variations of the Region Proposal Method were developed in the literature, and the goal with each one was to enhance the results of the one before.

   - Sliding Window Method: The first step of the sliding window detector is to apply a CNN on the training set that contains cropped and labeled objects; it generates a model that can identify the required objects. Next, the same CNN is used to classify the objects inside the image by receiving multiple parts cropped with a square-shaped frame known as a "Window" that scans the entire image with a constant stride. Finally, this step is repeated with different window sizes to find the most acceptable result [71]. The main disadvantage of this method is the high inference time when applied to point clouds because of the sparseness of the points.

   - Anchorless Detectors: The anchorless method avoids using many 3D anchors; instead, it follows the binary (foreground/background) segmentation-based detection settings, allowing models to be more memory efficient with lower computational cost. However, compared to the region proposal frameworks, the accuracy of these detectors is lower when detecting large objects (e.g., trucks, cars) and higher for small ones (e.g., cyclists, pedestrians).

- Hybrid Detectors: STD [57] is the general dual-stage approach that combines anchors and segmentation to generate region proposals.
5. Input Data Type: When it comes to the input data utilized in detection models, there are notably two different approaches; either base the solution only on LiDAR point clouds as the primary source of data or merge it with images collected by RGB cameras.
   - Various approaches rely on the first method because of the rich geometric information the LiDAR sensor provides. The LiDAR point clouds could transformed into BEVs by omitting the height value of the Z-axis; then applying on them 2D object detection mechanisms used for RGB images. Some models [63] process the point clouds under the structure of 3D voxels or pillar representations are usually more expensive in terms of hardware and time. Finally, other approaches operate directly on the raw point cloud data as it is [56,57].
   - The approaches [72–74] based on both sensing technologies detect objects in more complex scenarios like small and distant objects, which is impossible using only LiDAR sensors. The main advantage of using RGB cameras is the generation of dense pixel images over a significant distance (depending on the camera's performance). Still, it doesn't give any information about objects' depth (the distance). Combining the two data types allows taking advantage of the densely pixelated images generated by RGB cameras and the accurate depth provided by LiDAR.

   The usage of two different types of data will improve the accuracy of the models in the majority of cases, but it comes with many disadvantages:
   - Models require precise calibration and synchronization between the LiDAR and the camera sensors, which makes the accuracy of the solution extremely dependent on any changes to the sensor position or view angle.
   - These fusion solutions are usually slower than the LiDAR-only solutions due to the large number of images to be processed, the usage of dual-stage architectures, and the deployment of RPNs for bounding box generation.
   - These solutions are so dependent on the detection performance of the 2D object detectors, and they are not capable of using the 3D information to enhance the accuracy of the bounding boxes.
   - The approaches relying on extracting and combining the features of multiple views (e.g., MV3D) face the problem of information loss due to the inconsistency of the feature sizes across the BEV projection, the front view projection, and the camera image. Thus, they need to normalize their sizes, which affects the detection performance.

3.2   Challenges

The perception system requires a single or a group of LiDAR sensors that periodically scan and collect the three-dimensional space around it and store it in point cloud files [8]. Next, it extracts important information and classifies the data by their semantic meaning. The LiDAR technology provides 3D point clouds that represent the scenes around the object holding the sensor. However, some factors make this task of perception extremely challenging like:

- The vast diversity of environments changes each second, including the state of the weather. It has been proven in different studies [75–77]that fog and rain can negatively influence the performance of the LiDAR sensor, but the LiDAR could still generated results better than other sensing technologies (e.g. RADAR).
- Objects could be obscure partially or entirely by other objects or parts of other objects.
- The input shape and size of an object detected by a LiDAR sensor depends on the distance and angle from which the object was detected. As a result, the same entity can have different shapes and sizes, creating confusion when classifying the object.
- The performance of the LiDAR sensor is dependent on the entire driving domain.

All the factors mentioned above hinder the quality of service that LiDAR can deliver; therefore, multiple approaches have combined LiDAR with different sensing technologies like RGB cameras [78] and stereo cameras [79], RADAR [80], and ultrasonic sensors [81]. The combination of the LiDAR sensor and monocular cameras is considered the most adopted method of multi-sensing architecture because of the LiDAR's capability to provide depth information. In contrast, cameras collect information richer in texture [8,53,82,83].

Besides, object detection is an essential step for the autonomous vehicle process. It relies on the data collected from a LiDAR or a LiDAR and RGB cameras and a machine-learning algorithm to create prediction models or enhance the performance of older versions. However, although LiDAR sensors provide high-resolution three-dimensional maps under various lighting conditions; the recourse to these sensors raises new challenges:

- The data generated by LiDAR sensors are sparse and unstructured.
- The volume of the point clouds is large, and their processing requires powerful types of equipment since the features extraction and the object detection steps are expected to be performed in real-time.
- The processing units are resource-constrained since vehicles are equipped with a limited source of energy (the battery of the vehicle); thus, the use of efficient computational models to process the point clouds is required.

1. The data generated by LiDAR sensors are sparse and unstructured. 2. The volume of the point clouds is significant, and their processing requires powerful equipment since feature extraction, and object detection steps are expected to be performed in real-time. 3. The processing units are resource-constrained since vehicles are equipped with a limited energy source (for electric cars); thus, efficient computational models are required to process the point clouds .

4   Conclusion

In this paper, we presented the LiDAR technology, including its functioning mechanism, types, its various application in different fields. We also tried to sum up the main feature that could be extracted from the LiDAR point clouds, and the feature extractors used on this type of data. Our work can still be improved by presenting the different 3D detection methods used by different LiDAR models.

References

1. Sikander, G., Anwar, S.: Driver fatigue detection systems: a review (2018)
2. World Health Organization: Road traffic injuries (2021). https://www.who.int/news-room/fact-sheets/detail/road-traffic-injuries
3. infinitinews.com 2002 infiniti q45 press kit: Overview (2010). https://usa.infinitinews.com/en-US/releases/2002-infiniti-q45-press-kit
4. toyota.ie. Parking aids (2017). https://www.toyota.ie/discover-toyota/safety/parking-aids
5. Krafcik, J.: Waymo is opening its fully driverless service to the general public in phoenix (2020). https://blog.waymo.com/2020/10/waymo-is-opening-its-fully-driverless.html
6. Roriz, R., Cabral, J., Gomes, T.: Automotive lidar technology: a survey (2021)
7. Raj, T., Hanim Hashim, F., Baseri Huddin, A., Ibrahim, M.F., Hussain, A.: A survey on lidar scanning mechanisms (2020)
8. Fernandes, D., et al.: Point-cloud based 3D object detection and classification methods for self-driving applications: a survey and taxonomy (2021). https://www.sciencedirect.com/science/article/abs/pii/S1566253520304097
9. Chetouane, A., Mabrouk, S., Mosbah, M.: Traffic congestion detection: solutions, open issues and challenges. In: Jemili, I., Mosbah, M. (eds.) DiCES-N 2020. CCIS, vol. 1348, pp. 3–22. Springer, Cham (2020). https://doi.org/10.1007/978-3-030-65810-6_1
10. Thakur, R.: Scanning lidar in advanced driver assistance systems and beyond: building a road map for next-generation lidar technology (2016)
11. Arastounia, M.: Automated recognition of railroad infrastructure in rural areas from lidar data (2015)
12. Reed, M.D., Pottle, D.F.: An operational airborne lidar survey system using kinematic DGPS (1998)
13. De Blasiis, M.R., Di Benedetto, A., Fiani, M., Garozzo, M.: Assessing of the road pavement roughness by means of lidar technology (2020)
14. QCIS3. A free and open source geographic information system (2021). https://www.qgis.org/en/site/
15. Whitebox GAT: Whitebox geospatial Inc. (2020). https://www.whiteboxgeo.com
16. Fugro Viewer. Fugroviewer (2022). https://www.fugro.com/about-fugro/our-expertise/technology/fugroviewer
17. Saga GIS. Saga (2007). https://saga-gis.sourceforge.io/en/index.html
18. GRASS GIS. Geographic resources analysis support system (2019). https://grass.osgeo.org
19. Meshlab. Meshlab description (2016). https://www.meshlab.net

20. CloudCompare. 3D point cloud and mesh processing software open source project (2020). https://www.cloudcompare.org
21. FARO. Faro scene software (2022). https://www.faro.com/en/Products/Software/SCENE-Software
22. Cyclone, L.: Leica cyclone 3D point cloud processing software (2022). https://leica-geosystems.com/products/laser-scanners/software/leica-cyclone
23. TR Works. Products-and-solutions (2022). https://geospatial.trimble.com/products-and-solutions/trimble-realworks
24. B. Pointools. Point-cloud processing software (2022). https://www.bentley.com/en/products/brands/pointools
25. PointCap. Pointcap (2013). https://pointcab-software.com/en/
26. PointFuse. Pointfuse (2022). https://pointfuse.com
27. EdgeWise. Edgewise-building (2020). https://www.clearedge3d.com/edgewise-building/
28. Capturing Reality. Capturing reality (2020). https://www.capturingreality.com
29. Autodesk ReCap. Overview (2022). https://www.autodesk.com/products/recap/overview
30. Open Topography. Open topography (2021). https://opentopography.org/about
31. USGS earth Explorer. USGS earth explorer (2022). https://earthexplorer.usgs.gov
32. NOAA Digital Coast. NOAA digital coast (2022). https://coast.noaa.gov/digitalcoast/
33. National Ecological Observatory Network. National ecological observatory network (2019). https://www.neonscience.org
34. Geiger, A., Lenz, P., Stiller, C., Urtasun, R.: Welcome to the KITTI vision benchmark suite! (2022). https://www.cvlibs.net/datasets/kitti/
35. Hagen, K.: U.S. airborne lidar market top impacting factors (2016). https://medium.com/@kathleenhagen2/u-s-airborne-lidar-market-top-impacting-factors-b19def6781c4
36. Torres, G.: Drone photogrammetry vs. lidar (2021). https://wingtra.com/drone-photogrammetry-vs-lidar/
37. Gugliotta, G.: Into the light: how lidar is replacing radar as the archaeologist's map tool of choice (2015). https://www.theguardian.com/science/2015/jun/20/lidar-radar-archaeology-central-america
38. savetheredwoods. Save the redwoods league (2022). https://www.savetheredwoods.org
39. Rabatel, A., Deline, P., Jaillet, S., Ravanel, L.: Rock falls in high-alpine rock walls quantified by terrestrial lidar measurements: a case study in the Mont Blanc area (2008). https://agupubs.onlinelibrary.wiley.com/doi/full/10.1029/2008GL033424
40. Paulson, T.: Lidar shows where earthquake risks are highest (2001). https://www.seattlepi.com/local/article/LIDAR-shows-where-earthquake-risks-are-highest-1052381.php
41. Earlinet. A European aerosol research lidar network to establish an aerosol climatology: Earlinet (2019). https://www.earlinet.org/index.php?id=earlinet_homepage
42. Areté Associates. Areté associates (1976). https://arete.com
43. Grumman, N.: Airborne laser mine detection system (ALMDS) (2022). https://www.northropgrumman.com/what-we-do/air/airborne-laser-mine-detection-system-almds/
44. Kim, H., Choi, Y.: Location estimation of autonomous driving robot and 3D tunnel mapping in underground mines using pattern matched lidar sequential images (2021). https://www.sciencedirect.com/science/article/pii/S209526862100080X

45. Peter, G.: Lidar: making light work of mining (2020). https://www.miningreview. com/base-metals/lidar-making-light-work-of-mining/
46. Hsieh, H.-H., Hsu, C.-Y., Ke, P.-Y., Liu, G.-S., Lin, C.-P.: Appling lidar-based obstacle detection and wireless image transmission system for improving safety at level crossings (2015). https://ieeexplore.ieee.org/document/7389711
47. Gézero, L., Antunes, C.: Automated three-dimensional linear elements extraction from mobile lidar point clouds in railway environments (2019). https://www.mdpi. com/2412-3811/4/3/46
48. Arastounia, M.: An enhanced algorithm for concurrent recognition of rail tracks and power cables from terrestrial and airborne lidar point clouds (2017). https:// www.mdpi.com/2412-3811/2/2/8
49. Andani, M.T., Peterson, A., Munoz, J., Ahmadian, M.: Railway track irregularity and curvature estimation using doppler lidar fiber optics (2016). https://journals. sagepub.com/doi/abs/10.1177/0954409716660738
50. Neubert, M.: Extraction of railroad objects from very high resolution helicopter-borne lidar and ortho-image data (2008). https://www.semanticscholar.org/ paper/EXTRACTION-OF-RAILROAD-OBJECTS-FROM-VERY-HIGH-LIDAR-Neubert-Hecht/71a091fa368b817588b3c84cd0532b7447ca4d87
51. Stein, D., Spindler, M., Kuper, J., Lauer, M.: Rail detection using lidar sensors. Int. J. Sustain. Dev. Plan. **11**(1), 65–78 (2016)
52. Lim, K., Tuladhar, K.M.: Lidar: lidar information based dynamic v2v authentication for roadside infrastructure-less vehicular networks (2019). https://ieeexplore. ieee.org/document/8651684
53. Zamanakos, G., Tsochatzidis, L., Amanatiadis, A., Pratikakis, I.: A comprehensive survey of lidar-based 3D object detection methods with deep learning for autonomous driving (2021). https://www.sciencedirect.com/science/article/abs/ pii/S0097849321001321
54. Yang, Z., Sun, Y., Liu, S., Jia, J.: 3DSSD: point-based 3D single stage object detector (2020). https://ieeexplore.ieee.org/document/9156597
55. Zhou, D., et al.: Joint 3D instance segmentation and object detection for autonomous driving (2020). https://ieeexplore.ieee.org/document/9156967
56. Shi, S., Wang, X., Li, H.: PointRCNN: 3D object proposal generation and detection from point cloud (2019). https://arxiv.org/abs/1812.04244
57. Yang, Z., Sun, Y., Liu, S., Shen, X., Jia, J.: STD: sparse-to-dense 3D object detector for point cloud (2019). https://arxiv.org/abs/1907.10471
58. Meng, Q., Wang, W., Zhou, T., Shen, J., Van Gool, L., Dai, D.: Weakly supervised 3D object detection from lidar point cloud. In: Vedaldi, A., Bischof, H., Brox, T., Frahm, J.-M. (eds.) ECCV 2020. LNCS, vol. 12358, pp. 515–531. Springer, Cham (2020). https://doi.org/10.1007/978-3-030-58601-0_31
59. Ngiam, J.: StarNet: targeted computation for object detection in point clouds (2019). https://arxiv.org/abs/1908.11069
60. Shi, S., et al.: PV-RCNN: point-voxel feature set abstraction for 3D object detection (2020). https://arxiv.org/abs/1912.13192
61. Shi, S., et al.: PV-RCNN++: point-voxel feature set abstraction with local vector representation for 3D object detection (2021). https://link.springer.com/article/ 10.1007/s11263-022-01710-9
62. Chen, Q., Sun, L., Cheung, E., Yuille, A.: Every view counts: cross-view consistency in 3D object detection with hybrid-cylindrical-spherical voxelization (2020). https://proceedings.neurips.cc/paper/2020/hash/ f2fc990265c712c49d51a18a32b39f0c-Abstract.html

63. Lang, A.H., Vora, S., Caesar, H., Zhou, L., Yang, J., Beijbom, O.: PointPillars: fast encoders for object detection from point clouds (2019). https://arxiv.org/abs/1812.05784

64. Qi, C.R., Liu, W., Wu, C., Su, H., Guibas, L.J.: Frustum pointnets for 3D object detection from RGB-D data (2018). https://arxiv.org/abs/1711.08488

65. Wang, Z., Jia, K.: Frustum convnet: sliding frustums to aggregate local point-wise features for amodal 3D object detection (2019). https://ieeexplore.ieee.org/document/8968513

66. Zhao, X., Liu, Z., Hu, R., Huang, K.: 3D object detection using scale invariant and feature reweighting networks (2019). https://arxiv.org/abs/1901.02237

67. Shi, W., Rajkumar, R.: Point-GNN: graph neural network for 3D object detection in a point cloud (2020). https://arxiv.org/abs/2003.01251

68. Yang, F., Choi, W., Lin, Y.: Exploit all the layers: fast and accurate CNN object detector with scale dependent pooling and cascaded rejection classifiers (2016). https://ieeexplore.ieee.org/document/7780603

69. Liu, Y., Li, H., Yan, J., Wei, F., Wang, X., Tang, X.: Recurrent scale approximation for object detection in CNN (2017). https://arxiv.org/abs/1707.09531

70. Wu, X., Sahoo, D., Hoi, S.C.: Recent advances in deep learning for object detection (2020). https://www.sciencedirect.com/science/article/abs/pii/S0925231220301430

71. Teutsch, M., Kruger, W.: Robust and fast detection of moving vehicles in aerial videos using sliding windows (2015). https://ieeexplore.ieee.org/document/7301396

72. Xu, D., Anguelov, D., Jain, A.: PointFusion: deep sensor fusion for 3D bounding box estimation (2018). https://arxiv.org/abs/1711.10871

73. Vora, S., Lang, A.H., Helou, B., Beijbom, O.: PointPainting: sequential fusion for 3D object detection (2020). https://arxiv.org/abs/1911.10150

74. Shin, K., Kwon, Y.P., Tomizuka, M.: RoarNet: a robust 3D object detection based on region approximation refinement (2019). https://ieeexplore.ieee.org/abstract/document/8813895

75. Michaud, S., Lalonde, J.-F., Giguère, P.: Towards characterizing the behavior of lidars in snowy conditions (2015). https://www.semanticscholar.org/paper/Towards-Characterizing-the-Behavior-of-LiDARs-in-Michaud-Lalonde/341db91199379c6f0a2db2252e25967e1887c17b

76. Kutila, M., Pyykönen, P., Holzhüter, H., Colomb, M., Duthon, P.: Automotive lidar performance verification in fog and rain (2018). https://ieeexplore.ieee.org/document/8569624

77. Heinzler, R., Schindler, P., Seekircher, J., Ritter, W., Stork, W.: Weather influence and classification with automotive lidar sensors (2019). https://ieeexplore.ieee.org/document/8814205

78. Caltagirone, L., Bellone, M., Svensson, L., Wahde, M.: Lidar-camera fusion for road detection using fully convolutional neural networks (2019). https://www.sciencedirect.com/science/article/abs/pii/S0921889018300496

79. Dieterle, T., Particke, F., Patino-Studencki, L., Thielecke, J.: Sensor data fusion of lidar with stereo RGB-D camera for object tracking (2017). https://ieeexplore.ieee.org/document/8234267

80. Göhring, D., Wang, M., Schnürmacher, M., Ganjineh, T.: Radar/lidar sensor fusion for car-following on highways (2011). https://ieeexplore.ieee.org/document/6144918

81. Rosdi, M.H.A.B., Abdul Ghani, A.S.: Investigation on accuracy of sensors in sensor fusion for object detection of autonomous vehicle based on 2D lidar and ultrasonic sensor. In: Ab. Nasir, A.F., Ibrahim, A.N., Ishak, I., Mat Yahya, N., Zakaria, M.A., P. P. Abdul Majeed, A. (eds.) Recent Trends in Mechatronics Towards Industry 4.0. LNEE, vol. 730, pp. 761–770. Springer, Singapore (2022). https://doi.org/10.1007/978-981-33-4597-3_68
82. Arnold, E., Al-Jarrah, O.Y., Dianati, M., Fallah, S., Oxtoby, D., Mouzakitis, A.: A survey on 3D object detection methods for autonomous driving applications (2019). https://ieeexplore.ieee.org/document/8621614
83. Zhong, H., Wang, H., Wu, Z., Zhang, C., Zheng, Y., Tang, T.: A survey of lidar and camera fusion enhancement (2021). https://www.sciencedirect.com/science/article/pii/S1877050921005767

Real-Time Prediction of Off-Street Parking Spaces Based on Dynamic Resource Allocation and Pricing

Sana Ben Hassine[1]([✉]) [iD], Elyes Kooli[2], and Raafa Mraihi[3] [iD]

[1] Higher Institute of Finance and Taxation of Sousse, 4000 Sousse, Tunisia
sana.benhassine@ymail.com
[2] Higher Institute for Technological Studies of Ksar Hellal, 5070 Ksar Hellal, Tunisia
[3] Higher School of Business of Tunis, 2010 Manouba, Tunisia

Abstract. Due to rapid economic development, people's living standards continue to improve, causing the number of urban motor vehicles to rise. Nevertheless, as the number of motor vehicles continues to grow, it is becoming increasingly difficult to find a vacant parking space. This study proposes a new intelligent parking system based on a multi-agent approach and dynamic pricing in order to achieve more effective, convenient, and accurate parking space prediction effect. By selecting a path, the driver is guided to a parking lot with unoccupied spaces. The system assigns and reserves a vacant parking space based on the driver's utility that combines travel time, cruising time, walking to destination and parking cost. MATSim transport simulation platform is used to simulate drivers from off-street parking in Tunis city center. The numerical analysis, based on real data from Open Data Tunisia, demonstrates that the developed intelligent off-street parking system reduces traffic congestion, minimizes travel time, and utilizes parking space more efficiently during peak hours.

Keywords: microscopic simulation · intelligent parking · multi-agent system

1 Introduction

Parking is of crucial importance, given its effects on urban development, on the dynamics of the city center, and on travel conditions throughout the metropolitan area [1]. It is an essential daily need for residential areas, as well as for the proper functioning of shops and economic and social activities. Efficient parking management can better predict movement and thus improve the vehicle rotation. It also facilitates access to the city center, revitalizes business districts, and stimulates shopping and leisure [2]. Parking can be the most powerful instrument [3] that public authorities have in their possession to control traffic in dense urban areas.

Realization of the parking importance issues in the global context of urban transportation problems has led many cities to take measures to better manage the demand for travel [4]. Nowadays, efficient parking management strategies are vital in dense urban

I. Jemili et al. (Eds.): DiCES-N 2023, CCIS 2041, pp. 28–40, 2024.
https://doi.org/10.1007/978-3-031-52823-1_2

areas where parking is limited and congestion is intense. In the literature, the solutions proposed are often political or technological [5].

Currently, the main guidance method in Tunisia is to display static information signs to inform drivers about parking spaces and the route to them [6]. Then, arriving at the parking lot, it is impossible to predict parking spaces' availability, resulting in waste of driver's time. Researchers have conducted extensive study on induced parking spaces and parking prediction.

Zhang et al. [7] studied dynamic parking pricing to reach the optimum of the system. However, this study does not take into account the parking information effect obtained by detecting the parking occupancy rate. While, Qian and Rajagopal [8] model parking pricing as a stochastic control problem. Parking pricing is adjusted in real-time, depending on the parking occupancy. The latter is detected using sensors installed in the parking area. The parking occupancy rate is thus analyzed to forecast future demand and to determine the optimal parking pricing for the following period. Kotb et al. [9] present a new smart parking system based on smart reservation and pricing. The new system is based on mathematical modeling, employing linear mixed integer programming to reduce the total monetary cost for drivers and maximize the use of parking resources.

To plan parking lots and integrate urban parking systems, Yeh et al. [10] use streaming media servers with cloud computing technology and smart mobile devices. The system provided parking search, navigation, reservations, and car retrieval services. Vision-based monitoring is proposed by Tang et al. [11] as a low-cost and contactless method of managing parking services. The authors also presented an adaptive parking monitoring system that can detect parking occupancy in a flexible way. In order to test this system, a conventional microcomputer can be connected to a webcam to determine unoccupied parking spaces.

Jingyu et al. [12] used Lot technology to model the roads and main parking lots in order to search a more accurate parking space prediction effect. Adaptive genetic algorithms are also used to simulate and induce drivers. The shortest path for the driver to reach each parking lot are then determined. Mei et al. [13] combine the Fourier transform with the least squares support vector regression machine learning technique. The method can be used to predict the number of steps in a multi-step and single-step parking lot.

Considering the occupancy condition of three parking spaces, Bora et al. [14] suggest an intelligent parking guidance model. Multi-agent simulations were conducted on five scenarios and results were compared with regard to occupancy ratios, wasted time, and gases emissions. An algorithm and system implementation architecture for smartphone-based parking guidance are presented by Gao et al. [15] to alleviate parking issues and improve service efficiency. Parking selection is described as a multi-criteria decision. Shortest paths are determined using the Dijkstra algorithm.

In urban areas, Huang and Hsieh [16] develop a smart decision support system to guide available on-street parking. Sensors capture the parking pictures and send them back to the database server in a short timeframe. The best parking slots are recommended using two mathematical models. Xie et al. [17]. The authors use deep reinforcement learning in an automated valet parking environment to solve the problem of parking space allocation. Markov decision processes is used to formulate the allocation problem.

The aim of the study is to develop an intelligent off-street parking system. The paper is an effective tool to make the best use of limited parking resources, guide drivers to the selected parking lot and improve the system efficiency in dense urban areas. A model based on dynamic resource allocation and pricing, and multi-agent systems may be an adequate modeling approach. This paper selects vehicle running time, parking cost, walking time, and cruising time as the characteristic parameters of the utility function.

This research is structured as follows. Section 2 describes the intelligent off-street parking prediction system implementation. Section 3 defines the simulation environment, the input data, and the notation and formulation of the utility function. Section 4 is reserved to numerical simulation. Finally, Sect. 5 reports some conclusions.

2   Off-Street Parking Prediction System Based on Multi-agent System

Multi-agent systems play a decisive role in the management of the proposed off-street parking system. The functional aspect is illustrated by a parking procedure in a cooperative environment of agents (Fig. 1).

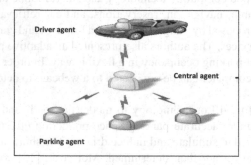

Fig. 1. Organizational structure of agents

Parking agents are responsible for forecasting and monitoring parking space occupancy, on the basis of which parking prices are determined. They are placed in the automatic barriers installed at the entrance and exit of off-street parking lots. The central agent is a central server for storing information from the area it manages. It plays the role of a central supervision entity, through direct interaction with parking agents.

2.1   Search for Available Parking Lot Spaces

Search for available parking spaces follows a hierarchical decision-making process. Drivers looking for parking spaces send queries to the central agent. With the assistance of parking agents, central agent assists drivers in finding a parking space according to their needs.

All pricing decisions are made by the parking agent, based on the condition of the parking lots and the users' requests. It continuously analyzes parking occupancy status, and determines parking prices according to a dynamic pricing scheme. All the information collected will be updated and stored in the parking agent's database. Upon registering the driver, the central agent contacts the parking agents located around the destination. Each proposal from the parking agents will be evaluated by the central agent.

2.2 Short Path Selection

The list of parking lots with unoccupied spaces appears instantly. Geographic Information Systems (GIS) produce maps that illustrate the location of the parking lot based on the driver's current location and his intended destination. Several details are displayed about each parking lot, including the name, type, price, walking time, and occupancy rate. Following the user's receipt of all the required information, he must take the initiative to select a parking space. The shortest path to selected parking is determined using the A* algorithm.

2.3 Parking Space Allocation

Allocation requests are sent to the central agent, who forwards them to the parking agent. This allocation is for a time period. Consequently, if any unexpected event occurs, like a car accident, the central agent must be notified in order to extend the stationing period. An allocation of parking spaces is necessary in order to avoid overcrowding in a parking lot at the same time. Absence of allocation is only an approximate indication of parking availability space.

3 Experiment

3.1 Simulation Environment

MATSim is a transportation network micro-simulation platform for large-scale applications. For our study, this software was selected as a model and simulation system for agents. MATSim is designed to run simulations repeatedly (Fig. 2). The simulation procedure is summarized in three main steps: execution, notation and replanning.

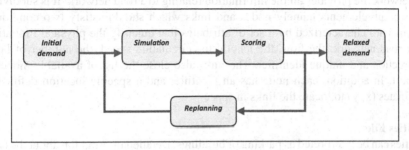

Fig. 2. MATSim simulation process [18]

Execution

In MATSim, demand is modeled individually for each agent. Modeling is done for a whole day, and it is called plan. Each agent independently generates a daily activity plan. This latter is a simple schedule of activities, their location in the study area and the preferred mode of transport to link these activities. All movement plans are then executed simultaneously in the simulator.

Notation

All executed plans are scored by a utility function. A utility function consists of several variables that differ among agents, resulting in heterogeneous decisions. A score is thus calculated for each execution plan.

The utility of a plan U_{plan} is calculated as the sum of the utilities of the activities $U_{act,i}$, the sum of the travel (dis)utilities $U_{travel,i}$ and the sum of the parking utilities $U_{parking,i}$ [17]:

$$U = \sum_{i=1}^{n} (U_{act,i} + U_{travel,i}) + \sum_{i=1}^{n} U_{parking,i} \tag{1}$$

Replanning

The replanning step is analogous to the mechanisms of mutation and selection. This adaptation process is reflected in iterations, until some form of equilibrium is reached. A fixed number of day plans are stored in each agent's memory, and each plan contains a daily activity chain and a utility value. Those activity plans with the highest utility scores are selected, and those with the lowest scores are deleted from the agents' memory.

3.2 Inputs Data

Several input files are required to construct a MATSim simulation, including road networks, installations, initial plans and simulation configurations. Files must respect the XML data format.

Network File

The network file provides all the information relating to a road network. It is subdivided into two sub-elements namely nodes and links which should satisfy two conditions. The links are characterized by a set of attributes that quantify the physical limitations of the road network: the flow, the length, the circulation speed, the number of lanes, the direction and unique identifier. The links also close the list of available modes of transport. In addition, each node has an identifier and a specific location defined by coordinates (x, y) to locate the links in space.

Facilities File

Facilities can be interpreted as parking or buildings. Detailed information about the types of activities that can be performed at specific locations (education or work) is provided in the facilities file, along with the facility's opening and closing times. Scheduling these hours prevents agents from transferring their activities overnight in order to avoid traffic jams.

Plan File

The plan file describes the simulated MATsim population and its travel demand. Each driver agent has a unique identity card (id) and holds a list of plans. These plans are a simple schedule of activities and travel stages. Activities are described by a list of attributes: type (home, work, education, shopping, leisure), location (geographical coordinates), start time, end time, and mode of transport (car, walk, bike, public transport, etc.).

Configuration File

The configuration file specifies all relevant settings and configurations for the tested scenario. The parameters of each module can be adjusted according to the specific needs of the scenario. Configuration files generally contain the following inputs: the number of iterations, the locations of input files, the types of strategies for agents, the types of adaptations to the plan, and the types of outputs to create.

3.3 Utility Function

To simplify the simulation, it is assumed that each movement activity is composed of two stages: a first from the origin o to the parking lot j, and a second from the parking lot j to the final destination d, for a single activity k (Table 1).

Table 1. Nomenclature

Simulation parameters	
P	Parking price
s	Parking stay duration
A_j^t	Parking availability at a time period t
C_j	Total capacity of parking lot j
l_{oj}	Distance to travel from the origin o to parking j
β_τ^{driv}	Marginal utility of time traveling
β_δ^{driv}	Marginal utility of distance traveled
β_μ	Marginal utility of money
β_τ^{cruis}	Marginal utility of cruising time inside the parking lots
$t_{oj}^{driv,t}$	Driving travel time t from the origin o to parking j
t_{jd}^{walk}	Time spent walking from parking j to final destination d
$t_{jd}^{cruis,t}$	Cruising time for parking j at a period time t

Let's consider two environments to be applied: static pricing with guidance (A2) and dynamic pricing with guidance (A3). The utility function MATSim Eq. (1), to be used in our simulation, can be rewritten as follows:

$$U_j^t = U_j^{driv,t} + U_j^{cruis,t} + U_j^{park,t} + U_j^{walk} \tag{2}$$

$$U_j^{driv,t} = \beta_\tau^{driv} \cdot t_{oj}^{driv} + \beta_\delta^{driv} \cdot l_{oj} \tag{3}$$

$$U_j^{cruis,t} = \beta_\tau^{cruis} \cdot t_j^{cruis,t} \tag{4}$$

$$U_j^{walk} = \beta_\tau^{walk} \times t_{jd}^{walk} \tag{5}$$

$$U_j^{park,t} = \beta_\mu \cdot s \cdot P_j^t = \beta_\mu \cdot s \cdot P_j \ln\left(\frac{C_j}{A_j^{t-1}}\right), \text{ such as: } A_j^t \neq 0 \tag{6}$$

$$U_j^t = \beta_\tau^{driv} \cdot t_{oj}^{driv,t} + \beta_\delta^{driv} \cdot l_{oj} + \beta_\tau^{cruis} \cdot t_j^{cruis,t} + \beta_\mu \cdot s \cdot P_j^t + \beta_\tau^{walk} \cdot t_{jd}^{walk} \tag{7}$$

3.4 Simulation Assumptions

A simulation is performed from the driver's current location to the chosen parking lot, along with walking time and parking costs. Besides, as part of the proposed algorithm, a number of factors are taken into account, such as search time and parking duration.

Two environments have been created in order to study the effect of dynamic pricing with guidance on the proposed off-street parking system. Real-world scenarios representing the current parking situation in Tunis city center are tested to implement and evaluate the suggested approach. The two environments have been compared. An environment with static pricing and guidance is described in the first notice (A2). An environment with dynamic pricing and guidance is described in the second notice (A3). During the simulation process, the underlying assumptions are taken into account. Let's consider:

- Vehicles are the only dynamic component of the road network.
- Parking locations, fees, and spaces are supervised by one parking manager.
- Drivers have access to real-time parking information such as price, available space, etc.
- Time value is assumed to be the same for all drivers.

4 Results and Discussions

The study area is generated from the road map, associated with the parking maps of downtown Tunis. This network includes constructed routes of 1361 links and 584 nodes. In addition, off-street parking of Tunis offers 6001 spaces. Simulated vehicles (randomly generated) number approximately 10000. Simulating a limited period, usually the morning peak, is the objective of the simulation.

4.1 Traffic State

A simulation day's number of vehicles can be seen in Fig. 3. As compared to the environment (A2), the environment (A3) reduces the number of vehicles in circulation proportionally. Parking occupancy allocation is not taken into account in (A2), unlike (A3). In this way, drivers may be directed to parking lots with a high occupancy rate, increasing congestion around them.

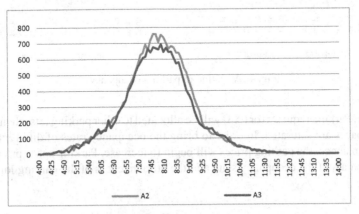

Fig. 3. Variation in vehicle numbers

During certain periods, such as 6:45 am to 9:25 am, the environment application (A2) can increase in vehicle flow. Nevertheless, it is estimated that (A3) would result in a reduction in road traffic of 7.62% on the simulation date. As a result, traffic has become less congested.

4.2 Parking Occupancy State

In Fig. 4, guidance with dynamic pricing is compared to guidance with static pricing for optimizing parking occupancy.

As an example, this figure shows how many cars are parked at Palmarium and Khartoum parking lots. Parking demand (A2) for the Palmarium parking is raised for the period from 6 am to 9 am. Nevertheless, by applying (A3), parked vehicles have been reduced for a similar period, until saturation has been reached. Unlike Khartoum parking, (A3) has an increase in occupancy in the early morning because parking demand is low.

(A3) reduce the number of vehicles in Palmarium by redirecting them to less crowded parking lots like Khartoum. While in (A2), drivers are guided to vacant parking spaces no matter what the occupancy rate is. Then, the saturated parking lots will be fully occupied. On the other hand, the occupancy rate in other districts is significantly lower. Parking occupancy balancing optimization is therefore required.

Parking prices can be accessed in real-time through an intelligent off-street parking system (Fig. 5), as a way to encourage drivers to switch parking lots based on parking

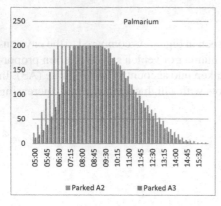
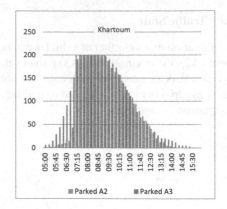

Fig. 4. Variation in parking occupancy

occupancy. Parking requests for (A3) will be allocated to other parking lots when the (A3) parking spaces are saturated. In order to bring the occupancy rates of different parking types into balance, the parking prices will begin to increase. Parking space pricing gives information about the occupancy state and the attractiveness of the parking lot.

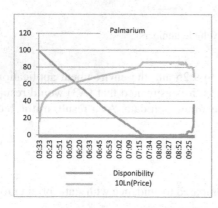
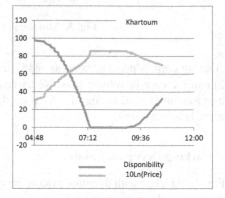

Fig. 5. Parking pricing elasticity

Figure 5 shows that parking pricing generally starts with a minimum value which can reach up to 0td. It is noted that it increases over time, following the decrease in vacant place number. Higher parking charges are levied in parking places with high occupancy. It stabilizes during peak hours takes a maximum value of up to 5td. Once the vehicle parked number decreases (availability rate rises), the parking pricing weakens. (A3) modifies prices to react quickly to variations in parking demand throughout the simulation. Dynamic prices with guidance optimize off-street parking occupancy.

4.3 Travel Time

On the simulation day, the time spent traveling by vehicles is defined as the travel time.

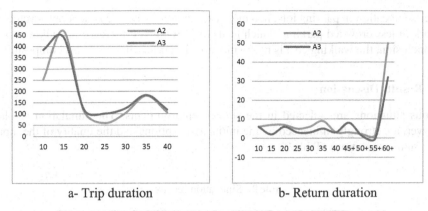

a- Trip duration   b- Return duration

Fig. 6. Travel time distribution

Number of vehicles passing between 5 min and 12 min in displacement increased, while those who passing between 12 min and 19 min were reduced, to resume ascending from 20 min (Fig. 6a). Based on this result, there is an average 12.3% reduction in travel time when (A3) is applied. Then, Parking congestion in the study area has reduced (vehicles are spread across all existing parking lots).

The time drivers spent leaving parking j and reaching o is shown in Fig. 6b. As a result of applying (A3), the travel time has increased somewhat. There is a reason for this, as (A3) may redirect drivers to parking lots that are less busy, but are further from their final destination. Travel time is likely to be extended in this situation.

4.4 Walking Time

Walking time describes the walking time elapsed by the driver from parking j to the final destination d.

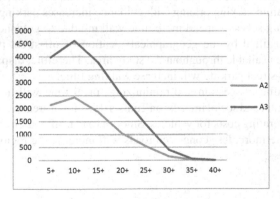

Fig. 7. Walking time variation

Walking time (Fig. 7) is estimated at 12.1 min on average for (A2) to 13.16 min for (A3). In fact, the increase in walking time is due to the spatial dispersion of the driver's allocation in parking lots. In a more explanatory way, (A3) encourages vehicles to park in less crowded parking, which leads to a significant increase in walking time. In conclusion, the walking cost is by far the most important in travel cost composition.

4.5 Results Discussion

Various situations are reflected in the studied environments. The simulation results, however, are strongly influenced by the initial assumptions and the quality of the input data (input generation) (Table 2).

Table 2. Simulation results

Indicators	Environment (A2)	Environment (A3)
Vehicle numbers	-	↘ 07.62%
Parking occupancy	-	↗ 05.00%
Travel time	-	↘ 12.03%
Walking time	-	↗ 20.66%

Dynamic pricing and guidance alleviate urban congestion according to simulation results. The driver will be directed to a parking lot whose occupancy rate is lower once the parking lots around their destination are full. As a result, congestion around parking lots shifts to adjacent areas. Test results were as expected. A Shoup [19] study found that vehicles flow searching for available parking space account for 30% of traffic flow. Therefore, dynamic pricing with guidance environment (A3) generates proportionally less fluid traffic than static pricing with guidance environment (A2).

In addition, guidance coupled with dynamic pricing reduces drivers' travel time. This result is closely related to the number of vehicles on the road network (road congestion). Furthermore, dynamic parking pricing with guidance increases parking occupancy.

Users of parking services spend more time walking due to guidance with dynamic pricing. This is justified by the geographical location of off-street parking. A wide variety of them are available throughout the study area. Therefore, dispatching driver to an unsaturated off-street parking will increase walking time.

Alleviating traffic congestion and minimizing travel time will have positive economic, environmental and social impacts on Tunis's downtown area. A shorter travel time results in lower operating costs for vehicles. Smooth road traffic often leads to increased productivity. Furthermore, less congested roads will increase the region's accessibility and competitiveness.

5 Conclusion

In urban areas, off-street parking lots, including building accessorial parking and public parking lots, are important resources. Nevertheless, a waste of parking resources results from an unreasonable allocation of off-street parking lots (density and layout of parking spaces). In consequence, analyzing parking supply and demand, parking management strategies, and other factors needs to be considered when allocating off-street parking lots.

In order to increase off-street parking's benefits to society and economy, it is necessary to adopt some appropriate management strategies (parking charging, technology, parking sharing, etc.) to encourage more drivers to park there. In this paper, an intelligent off-street parking system based on dynamic resource allocation and pricing is proposed to further improve the service level.

The present study models the roads, nodes, and main parking lot. Off-street parking lots are considered as virtual facilities, and the path from an intersection node to the associated parking lot is considered as a virtual path. Based on the simulation calculation, an unoccupied parking space must be found and the shortest route to reach each parking lot is determined.

In this paper, a multi-agent approach is presented that dynamically allocates parking spaces. The model is trained and predicted using data from Tunis city center. Utility function parameters selected for this study were vehicle running time, parking cost, walking time, and cruising time.

According to experimental results, a parking lot induction method based on a multi-agent approach and dynamic pricing can effectively select and allocate parking resources. A shortest path is combined with the agent's selection to guide the driver to the most optimal parking lot.

References

1. Ben Hassine, S., Harizi, R., Mraïhi, R.: Intelligent parking management system by multi-agent approach: the case of urban area of Tunis. In: 3rd International conference on advanced Logistic and Transport, Hammamat, Tunisia. IEEE (2014)
2. Ben Hassine, S., Kooli, E., Mraihi, R.: Multi-agent smart parking system with dynamic pricing. In: Abraham, A., Hanne, T., Gandhi, N., Manghirmalani Mishra, P., Bajaj, A., Siarry, P. (eds.) SoCPaR 2022. LNNS, vol. 648, pp. 781–790. Springer, Cham (2023). https://doi.org/10.1007/978-3-031-27524-1_76
3. Said, L.B., Syafey, I.: The scenario of reducing congestion and resolving parking issues in Makassar City Indonesia. Case Stud. Transp. Policy 9(4), 1849–1859 (2021)
4. Ben Hassine, S., Mraïhi, R., Kooli, E., Lachiheb, A.: Modelling parking type choice behavior. Int. J. Transp. Sci. Technol. 17, 430–442 (2022)
5. Chen, J., Yang, G.: Off-street parking. In: International Encyclopedia of Transportation, pp. 285–288 (2021)
6. Ben Hassine, S., Mraïhi, R., Kooli, E.: Driver's parking choice behavior study. In: 12th International Colloquium of Logistics and Supply Chain Management Logistiqua. IEEE, IUT de Montreuil, Université Paris8, France (2019)
7. Zhang, X., Yang, H., Huang, H.-J.: Improving travel efficiency by parking permits distribution and trading. Transp. Res. Part B 45, 1018–1034 (2011)
8. Zhen, Q., Rajagopal, R.: Optimal occupancy-driven parking pricing under demand uncertainties and traveler heterogeneity: a stochastic control approach. Trans. R. 67, 144–165 (2014)
9. Kotb, A.O., Shen, Y.-C., Zhu, X., Huang, Y.: Iparker-a new smart carparking system based on dynamic resource allocation and pricing. IEEE Trans. Intell. Transp. Syst. 17(9), 1–11 (2016)

10. Yeh, H.T., Chen, B.C., Wang, B.X.: A city parking integration system combined with cloud computing technologies and smart mobile devices. Eurasia J. Math. Sci. Technol. Educ. **5**, 1231–1242 (2016)
11. Tang, Y., et al.: Real-time detection of surface deformation and strain in recycled aggregate concrete-filled steel tubular columns via four-ocular vision. Robot. Comput.-Integr. Manuf. **59**, 36–46 (2019)
12. Liu, J., Jing, W., Sun, L.: Control method of urban intelligent parking guidance system based on Internet of Things. Comput.-Commun. **153**, 279–328 (2020)
13. Mei, Z., Zhang, W., Zhang, L., Wang, D.: Real-time multistep prediction of public parking spaces based on Fourier transform–least squares support vector regression. Intell. Transp. Syst. **24**, 68–80 (2020)
14. Dogaroglu, B., Caliskanelli, S.P., Tanyel, S.: Comparison of intelligent parking guidance system and conventional system with regard to capacity utilization. Sustain. Cities Soc. **74**, 103152 (2021)
15. Gao, H., Yun, Q., Ran, R., Ma, J.: Smartphone-based parking guidance algorithm and implementation. Intell. Transp. Syst. **25**, 412–422 (2021)
16. Huang, Y.-H., Hsieh, C.-H.: A decision support system for available parking slots on the roadsides in urban areas. Expert Syst. Appl. **205**, 117668 (2022)
17. Xie, J., He, Z., Zhu, Y.: A: DRL based cooperative approach for parking space allocation in an automated valet parking system. Appl. Intell. **53**, 5368–5387 (2022)
18. Waraich, R.A., Dobler, C., Axhausen, K.W.: Modelling parking search behaviour with an agent-based approach. In: 13th International Conference on Travel Research Behaviour (IATBR), Toronto (2012)
19. Shoup Donald, C.: Cruising for parking. Transp. Policy **13**, 479–486 (2006)

Shared Micro-mobility: Technologies, Challenges and Prospects of Using Collected Data

Rania Swessi[1](✉) and Zeineb EL Khalfi[2]

[1] Univ. Bordeaux, LaBRI, UMR 5800, Bordeaux, France
rania.swessi@u-bordeaux.fr
[2] LINEACT CESI, Campus de Bordeaux, Bordeaux, France

Abstract. Electric micro-vehicles including scooters, bicycles, and mopeds are gaining popularity as a preferred shared mode of transportation due to their environmental sustainability and cost-effectiveness. However, despite their numerous benefits, these micro-mobility services face several challenges that may limit their adoption. In this paper, we provide a comprehensive discussion of shared micro-mobility services as well as the associated challenges, including maintenance difficulties, infrastructure regulation, safety concerns, and imbalance issues. We also explore the potential solutions that have been implemented to address these challenges and the available datasets that can be used to optimize micro-mobility services.

Keywords: Micro-mobility devices · Connected micro-mobility · Micro-mobility datasets · Challenges · Service optimization

1 Introduction

Shared micro-mobility services have become increasingly popular in recent years as a flexible and sustainable alternative to traditional transportation options [14, 25, 39]. Companies like Bird, Lime, and Voi offer electric bikes, scooters, and other small vehicles for short trips in urban areas. These services are particularly useful for tourists, workers, and anyone seeking a quick and convenient transportation mode for their daily needs [13]. In addition to being cost-effective and affordable with low rental fees, micro-mobility services are eco-friendly, requiring significantly less energy to operate than traditional cars. Furthermore, they help alleviate traffic congestion and parking demand in urban areas, making them a more practical and efficient transportation option [39]. However, the reliability of these services is often challenged by various issues, such as maintenance difficulties, infrastructure regulation, safety, and imbalance problems [23, 26, 38, 40]. These issues can severely impact user satisfaction and company revenue. Therefore, it is crucial for micro-mobility operators to implement effective strategies to enhance the services and the overall user experience. Fortunately, researchers have shown that collected data from shared micro-mobility systems, such as trips, locations, and traffic data, can help solve these problems. For example, trip data or location can be utilized to optimize fleet placement and reduce maintenance costs [37]; while vehicle sensor data or traffic data can be used to identify collision risks and improve user safety [22, 26].

This paper offers a comprehensive analysis of micro-mobility services, with a particular focus on the devices and technologies used for communication between them. It presents a detailed overview of the challenges facing these services, with the existing datasets that can be leveraged to address them. By synthesizing the latest research and insights, it offers practical guidance for researchers and practitioners in this field. In addition, we perform an analysis of a real-world dataset obtained from the Bird company's micro-vehicle fleet usage in Bordeaux to determine the key factors that can enhance the services and improve the overall user experience.

The remainder of this paper is organized as follows: In Sect. 2, we introduce the micro-mobility service, including the different modes that are commonly used and the technologies that enable their communication. Section 3 provides an overview of the challenges faced by micro-mobility services, while Sect. 4 outlines how collected data from micro-mobility services can be used to solve these problems and optimize the services.

2 Overview of Shared Micro-mobility Services and Technologies

As the demand for urban transportation solutions has increased, shared micro-mobility services have emerged as a viable and sustainable option for short-distance trips. To support the efficient operation of these services, various communication methods are used to enable real-time tracking, monitoring, and management of the micro-mobility devices. This ensures that users have access to accurate and up-to-date information on vehicle availability, location, and route planning. Additionally, it enables operators to effectively manage and maintain their fleets, optimize vehicle allocation and charging, and respond quickly to any issues or incidents. This section will cover the characteristics of the commonly used devices in shared micro-mobility services, as well as the communication technologies that enable their effective deployment and operation.

2.1 Micro-mobility Devices

In recent years, the availability of shared micro-mobility services has greatly expanded, covering a variety of frequently used modes like bicycles and e-scooters [1, 11]. These modes of transportation differ in terms of design, cost, and operation mode. Figure 1 shows an example of micro-mobility devices, including e-scooters, e-bikes, e-mopeds, and segways.

Bikes are typically the most affordable and widely available mode of shared micro-mobility transportation. They are simple to use and provide a low-impact workout. Electric bikes, or pedelecs, on the other hand, offer a smoother ride thanks to a pedal assist feature that makes it easier for users to travel further and faster. A speed-pedelec (S-pedelec) is a type of electric bike that is designed to provide assistance up to higher speeds, typically up to 45 km/h, and may have different legal requirements than traditional e-bikes. Electric scooters are also common and practical to use, with their straightforward design making it simple for users to park them anywhere in free-floating systems. Although more expensive and requiring a valid driver's license to operate, electric mopeds offer a more powerful and effective form of transportation. Finally, electric skateboards and segways are the newer additions to the micro-mobility market, offering unique and fun transportation modes that are popular among young adults; however, they are not yet widely available for shared use. In the end, a person's choice of transportation depends on their preference, budget, and intended use.

E-Scooter   E-Bike/S-Pedelec   E-Moped   Segway

Fig. 1. Example of micro-mobility devices

These shared micro-vehicles allow users to rent vehicles for a limited time at an affordable cost. Most shared micro-mobility services are accessed through a mobile app that lets users find nearby vehicles, unlock them with their phones, and pay for their use. Shared micro-mobility services can be classified into two main categories: fleet services (where the vehicles are managed and provided by a company) and peer-to-peer services (where individual vehicle owners make their vehicles available to other users for a fee) [9,32]. Fleet services can be both docked and dockless, with or without charging stations, depending on the type of vehicle.

Table 1 represents a comparison of micro-mobility devices, their features, and specifications like average weight, power supply, range (the distance that the device can travel in a single charge), legal requirements, etc. The values presented in the table are indicative averages and may not accurately represent the precise specifications of each micro-mobility device.

Table 1. Micro-mobility devices and their features

Feature	Device				
	E-scooter	E-bike	S-pedelec	E-moped	Segway
Average weight (kg)	10–25	15–25	30–35	30–70	50–60
Max speed (km/h)	25	25	45	45	20
Operable pedal	no	possible	yes	possible	no
Power supply (watts)	250–500	250–750	500–750	500–2000	400–800
Range (km/h)	40–100	40–80	50–100	50–100	20–30
Average charging time	4–8 h	3–6 h	3–6 h	4–8 h	4–8 h
Occupants	single rider	single rider	single rider	multiple riders	single rider
Legal requirements	none	none	license/helmet	license/helmet	possible
Age requirements	14–16	14–16	>16	>16	14–16

2.2   Micro-mobility Companies

There are several shared micro-mobility companies that have gained popularity around the world, with some of the most well-known being:

1. **Bird** provides electric scooters and bikes and operates in around 50 metropolitan areas across the United States, 14 cities in Europe, and 3 cities in the Middle East. Their micro-vehicles are available for short-term rentals through the Bird mobile app and are designed to be a sustainable transportation option. Bird's electric scooters and bikes are designed to be lightweight and easy to use, with a top speed of 32 km/h and a range of up to 50 km/h on a single charge [3].
2. **Lime** provides electric bikes, scooters, and mopeds in over 100 cities worldwide. Lime's electric vehicles are designed to be easy to use and are equipped with safety features such as lights and brakes [13, 17].
3. **Voi** is a Swedish shared micro-mobility company that provides a variety of electric vehicles, including bikes, scooters, and mopeds. Voi's mobile app is also designed with sustainability in mind, with features such as a carbon footprint calculator that shows users how much CO_2 is saved [34].
4. **Spin** is a popular shared micro-mobility company that provides electric scooters, bikes, and e-assist bikes. It operates in over 70 cities worldwide, including Europe, Canada, and the United States. Spin's micro-vehicles are designed to be reliable, with a focus on safety and durability. Spin's mobile application is also user-friendly, with clear instructions on where to locate and how to unlock the fleet, as well as helpful riding safety tips [31].

Various systems are used by micro-mobility companies to handle their fleets. Docking is a common system in which vehicles are picked up and dropped off at designated stations. These stations can be fixed physical stations or virtual stations. Virtual stations refer to well-defined zones without physical boundaries, with an obligation to park the fleet inside these zones. Alternatively, the dockless system allows users to park vehicles anywhere within a specific operating zone. Some companies use a hybrid system that offers both docked and undocked parking options. The choice of a system depends on several factors, such as the city's size and metropolis, user demand, and regulatory requirements. Each system has its own advantages and disadvantages, making it essential for companies to assess their needs before deciding on the most suitable option.

Micro-mobility companies also adapt to the specific needs and expectations of their customers and focus on specific purposes such as Bird for leisure, Lime for work, and Voi for tourism [4,21]. However, this choice can also depend on various factors, including personal needs, distances, available transportation options, traffic conditions, and individual preferences.

2.3   Technologies Used in Connected Micro-mobility Devices

Shared micro-mobility vehicles, such as e-scooters, e-bikes, and e-mopeds, are typically equipped with wireless communication systems, such as embedded SIM cards, Global Positioning System (GPS) receivers, and sensors [6,8,24]. These technologies not only allow companies to track the vehicles' location and condition, but they also enable direct communication between the vehicles using short-range or low-power technologies such as Bluetooth, Zigbee, LoRa, or Wi-Fi [5,33,36]. Some shared micro-mobility vehicles can also be equipped with Vehicle-to-Vehicle (V2V) technology for short-range and direct communication. It enables the exchange of information between vehicles and can be used for collision avoidance, traffic optimization, and platooning. This technology can be especially useful in densely populated areas where there is a high demand for short-distance transportation.

To connect micro-mobility vehicles to the internet or to the central control system, cellular communication technologies such as 4G and 5G can be used for long-range communication [28]. 4G allows for high-speed remote communication, enabling operators to monitor in real-time the status of vehicles, such as their battery level, speed, track status, and other key components. With the arrival of 5G, the infrastructure is expected to further improve road safety with a comprehensive vision of traffic and roads in real-time, allowing for more advanced safety features [28]. Additionally, 5G will enable faster and more reliable communication for monitoring, control, and management of micro-mobility fleets, which can lead to more efficient operations and better overall user experience. Some other technologies including Near Field Communication (NFC), or QR codes can also be used to connect the device to the user's mobile phone or unlock the fleet [8]. Table 2 represents a comparison of communication technologies used in shared micro-mobility systems.

Regarding shared micro-mobility companies, Bird and Lime, use a combination of communication technologies including Wi-Fi, Bluetooth, and cellular communication depending on the region's infrastructure and local conditions [33]. Ultimately, the choice of communication technologies depends on each company's needs, the availability, and quality of wireless networks in a given region, the transmission range, and local regulatory requirements. Companies may also adopt new technologies as they evolve to meet the changing needs of users and improve the overall experience of shared micro-mobility.

Table 2. Comparison of communication technologies in micro-mobility

Technology	Range/power consumption	Data transfer rate	Communica- tion mode	Typical use case
Bluetooth	10 m/low	1 Mbps	device-to-device	data tracking and control
Wi-Fi	100 m/moderate	10 Gbps	device-to-hub/router	data exchange, navigation, and remote management
Zigbee	100 m/low	250 kbps	device-to-device/to hub	data exchange, tracking and control
LoRa	10 km/low	50 kbps	device-to-device/gateway	track location and usage /monitoring in real-time
V2V	300 m/low	27 Mbps	device-to-device	collision avoidance, traffic optimization, and platooning
4G/5G	6–10 km /high	10 Gbps	device-to-cellular networks	high-speed data transfer, and remote control

3 Challenges Facing the Micro-mobility Industry: An Overview

The field of micro-mobility faces various challenges related to infrastructure, regulation, system imbalance, and safety. One of the major issues is the lack of proper infrastructure for micro-mobility vehicles, such as bike lanes, parking areas, and charging stations [19,20,35]. This makes it difficult for users to use and park their vehicles safely and conveniently, which increases the number of improperly parked fleets. Another challenge is the need for regulations that balance the benefits of micro-mobility with issues of public safety, privacy, and property rights. For example, some cities have imposed restrictions on the number of shared micro-vehicles allowed on their streets or required companies to share private data on their operations. Additionally, safety is a concern as accidents involving micro-mobility vehicles have increased. [30]. This requires the implementation of safety measures such as helmets and educational campaigns for both users and drivers.

Micro-mobility vehicles require regular maintenance to remain secure and in excellent operating condition [19]. For example, the batteries in electric micro-vehicles need to be recharged regularly, but their life span can decrease over time, reducing their capacity and performance. Tires on rubber-tired vehicles can suffer damage, punctures, and wear, which also affects their safety and performance. Brakes and brake pads should be checked and replaced if needed. Electrical components may also need maintenance to function properly, and all vehicles experience general wear and tear over time, requiring repair and maintenance. These maintenance issues can be costly and time-consuming, especially for individual owners of micro-mobility vehicles [19].

Regarding the communication technologies in micro-mobility systems, they pose potential security risks. For example, bike and scooter companies utilize a combination of Bluetooth and internet connections to communicate with users' mobile phones and central servers. This can make them vulnerable to hacking and the potential mobilization of numerous vehicles in an urban setting. The authors in [28,29], propose a wireless communication technology designed to enable long-range communication between devices with low power consumption, namely Low-Power Wide-Area Network (LPWAN). This technology can improve safety and reduce accidents.

Fleet maldistribution and system imbalance are major challenges that affect the availability and accessibility of micro-mobility services and, ultimately, user satisfaction [15,16,23,40]. In the case of dockless systems, fleet maldistribution can result in certain regions or zones being underserved while other areas are oversaturated with vehicles. In physical dock-based systems, system imbalance can lead to empty or full docking stations, which can inconvenience users and undermine the usefulness of the service. When docking stations are completely empty, users are unable to access the service and may be forced to seek alternative transportation methods. On the other hand, when docking stations are completely full, users may have difficulty finding a parking spot, which can result in frustration and discourage further usage of the service. These issues have a negative impact on customer satisfaction, with customers suffering from unfavorable effects like longer wait times, farther travel in finding fleets, and difficulty accessing the service. Furthermore, a decrease in service quality could result in lower customer adoption rates and revenue for the company. To overcome these challenges, micro-mobility providers must develop effective strategies to optimize the distribution of fleets and the management of docking stations while leveraging real-time data and analytics to improve the overall user experience.

4   How Can Micro-mobility Datasets Be Beneficial?

Data gathering from shared micro-mobility systems can help solve some issues with user satisfaction and safety, while also significantly improving services. For example, trajectory data or location data can be used to optimize fleet placement, reducing imbalance issues and improving user accessibility. Vehicle sensor data or traffic can be used to detect collision risks and potential accidents, enabling preventive measures to reduce these risks and ensure user safety. In addition, data on users' usage patterns can be used to improve pricing models, service offerings, and user satisfaction.

4.1   Using Data for Better Problem-Solving and Services

The use of collected data from shared micro-mobility systems may offer many opportunities to improve the quality and efficiency of services while ensuring a more satisfying and safer user experience. Table 3, presents a comprehensive overview of datasets used by articles to address micro-mobility challenges, including information on data availability statements, collection years, system and fleet type, targeted issues, and data analysis country.

Table 3. Used datasets for addressing micro-mobility challenges

Ref	Data type	Statement	Year	Fleet type	Problem	Country
[15]	trip/weather	public	2015–2017	docked bike	imbalance	Korea
[18]	trip	public	2013–2016	docked bike	imbalance	NewYork
[16]	trip/weather	public	2016	docked bike	imbalance	China
[25]	trip	private	2019	dockless scooter	relocation	Canada
[12]	trip/weather	private	2019	dockless scooter	relocation	Korea
[37]	trip	open	2019	dockless bike	maintenance/relocation	NewYork
[41]	trip	open	2017	dockless bike	maintenance/relocation	China
[14]	trip/weather	private	2020	dockless scooter	relocation	Korea
[26]	sensor	open	2020–2021	dockless scooter	infrastructure/safety	Italy
[38]	trip/weather	public	2013–2017	docked pedelec	maintenance cost	NewYork
[7]	trip	open	2018–2019	dockless scooter	infrastructure/safety	Texas
[22]	region/traffic	private	2018	dockless scooter	relocation	Turkey
[2]	sensor/traffic	private	2015	docked bike	station placement	US
[10]	crashes/trips	private	2019–2021	dockless	infrastructure safety	Italy
[27]	trip/weather	private	2020	dockless scooter	relocation	Chicago

The authors in [15,18], describe a method for solving placement problems in physical dock-based systems by utilizing trip data and advanced deep-learning architectures. The solution relies on predicting user demand and using graph networks to model the connections between stations as nodes and the dependencies between them as edges, with the ultimate goal of balancing the fleet. In [16], the researchers propose a reinforcement learning[1] framework based on recorded trips between docked stations. This would help the system find a good balance. The solution consists of loading from a blocked predicted station and unloading at an empty station. In [12,25], the researchers use real-world trip data, taking into account weather and temporal criteria, to enhance the fleet locations and decrease the research time to find a fleet. They represented the demand using heatmap images as a strategy to identify future frequent areas. They employed machine learning forecasting techniques to predict the demand density at each hour within the operational zone. This strategy can help operators choose the best locations for their fleets and enhance the user experience by analyzing demand density images. To address both maintenance and redistribution challenges, the authors, in [37], propose a reinforcement learning-based multi-agent system that enhances micro-vehicle availability while minimizing the need for relocation and battery replacements. This solution is designed using a trip dataset and is capable of improving operational efficiency. In [41], the researchers prove the effectiveness of initiating users to balance dockless systems and aggregate low-battery fleet together, saving the cost of maintenance. They

---

[1] Reinforcement learning is a branch of machine learning that involves the training of artificial agents to interact with their environments and learn the best actions to take using a deep neural network to increase reward and solve the problem.

propose a prediction tool capable of estimating user demand from recorded trips within an area using machine learning. In [14], the authors show that weather data can be used to predict how many users will want to use dockless systems. The solution can increase user satisfaction by minimizing the research time required to find a fleet.

To enhance micro-mobility safety as well as improve infrastructure, authors in [26], propose a safety-based efficiency indicator for urban areas, using a data envelopment analysis. This indicator allows evaluation of the safety efficiency for each studied area according to factors such as road intersections, vehicle speed, and the presence of bicycle lanes. The authors, in [38], focus on the development of an efficient prediction machine learning model that predicts the demand for pedelec use every 48 h and an optimal route plan for pedelec battery charging using real-world datasets. In [7], a method is presented for estimating street segment-level e-scooter flows using an open-source dataset that includes millions of trip origins and destinations. The authors prove that the proposed model can help cities better support the emerging shared micro-mobility service. Researchers, in [22], suggest a decision support system for e-scooter sharing systems that helps dynamically place e-scooters in urban areas where they are required. The goal of this system is to provide select options by combining real-time social media data with traffic density information and region data given by the multi-criteria analysis made using the Analytical Hierarchy Process (AHP). In [2], a station placement strategy is proposed in order to determine the best locations for 5 new bike-sharing stations in Fargo, North Dakota. The workflow combines a geographic information system (GIS), level of traffic stress (LTS) ratings, and location-allocation optimization models. Authors in [10] highlight the inefficiency of ad-hoc planning in developing safe infrastructure for micro-mobility, which is essential for creating climate-friendly, sustainable, and livable cities. They propose an automated network planning process that utilizes data from various empirical sources, including existing infrastructure networks, bicycle crashes, and trip data from Bird company. The modeling framework presented in the study is applied specifically to the city of Turin, Italy, but it can be extended to other cities as long as similar data is available. It is able to create new cycling tracks that prioritize both travel demand and cycling safety and can be integrated into the existing infrastructure. The authors, in [27], focus on redistribution fleet optimization by predicting user demand using a trip dataset. The solution can help operators pick the ideal areas for fleet deployment according to user needs. Additionally, it can be adapted to any redistribution strategy and can be used in various ways like reducing collision risks in areas where the model predicts high demand or optimizing pricing strategies by analyzing the number of future demands.

This last solution and the majority of solutions proposed to address micro-mobility issues such as relocation problems, infrastructure safety, or mainte nance costs rely on predicting user demand using advanced machine learning techniques. By leveraging this prediction, operators can optimize their services to better align with user needs and improve overall satisfaction. To accomplish this, data collected from shared micro-mobility systems, such as trip data, fleet positions, and infrastructure-related data, is processed using data science, data cleaning, and analysis techniques to prepare it for modeling. In this context, data visualization techniques can also be used to help in identifying other influential factors that should be prioritized in predicting user demand, like weather or traffic data. Through visualization, patterns, and trends within the data can be more easily identified, leading to a better understanding of the complex relationships between different variables.

4.2 A Review of a Real-World Micro-mobility Dataset (Bordeaux, 2021/2022)

We are delighted to collaborate with Bird [3], a leading operator in the micro-mobility space, to analyze their recent dataset on self-service fleet usage. This dataset provides a unique opportunity to explore real-world mobility trends in the city of Bordeaux, France, and address micro-mobility challenges, including user satisfaction and fleet availability. However, the dataset is not yet publicly available due to privacy concerns. In this section, we present the features of this dataset as well as strategies for leveraging it to improve service quality and meet user needs. Figure 2 shows the operating zone in Bordeaux, which covers a 36.56 Km^2 area and includes more than 100 virtual stations for e-bikes and e-scooters.

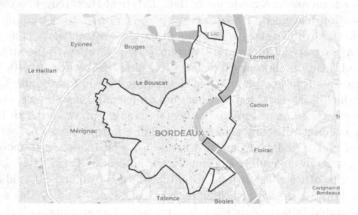

Fig. 2. Bird's operating area in Bordeaux city

Bird is one of the companies that rely on virtual stations to park its fleets in Bordeaux for regulatory reasons, in which users are obligated to park in well-defined georeferenced areas without physical boundaries with a radius of 15 m [3].

Bird provides us with a trip dataset for electric scooters and bikes that have been recorded, with the beginning and ending GPS positions collected in the city of Bordeaux. It includes over 71 thousand recorded trips between arrival and departure stations over the twelve 2021 months and the three winter months of 2022. Each transaction record includes the following details:

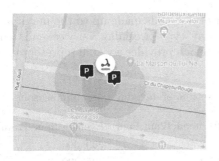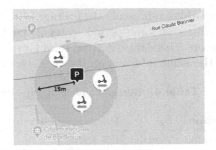

Fig. 3. Example of Bird virtual station

- Trip ID (Object): refers to the trip identifier.
- Vehicle checks out/in time (Object): refers to the date of reservation and the return of the fleet.
- Start and End position latitudes and longitudes (Float64): refers to the precise GPS start and end positions of the trip.

A list of fixed virtual stations is also given because trips are recorded with the exact GPS departure and arrival position rather than the virtual station to which they belong. This list includes the latitudes and longitudes positions and the identifier of the station.

The graphs shown in Fig. 4 illustrates the average demand (number of trips) for Bird's micro-mobility services during different times of the day across different seasons.

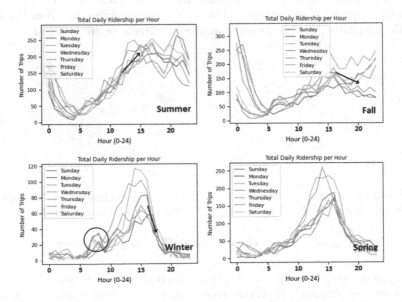

Fig. 4. Average demand for each season by hour and day (from Bird's data)

Table 4 represents the average number of demands made up to the maximum during each time period, categorized by day type (weekday vs. weekend) and season. This data is derived from Graph 4, which provides a visual representation of the same information.

Table 4. Average number of trips by the time of day, day type, and season

Season	Day	Morning(5am–12pm)	Afternoon(12pm–6pm)	Evening(6pm–12am)
Summer	Weekday	132–180	215–230	200–300
	Weekend	90–175	187–240	225–300
Fall	Weekday	70–150	120–150	100–300
	Weekend	60–100	140–150	120–160
Winter	Weekday	45–80	85–120	40–50
	Weekend	35–40	60–80	35–40
Spring	Weekday	100–175	137–250	75–100
	Weekend	60–100	100–180	75–100

As expected, the demand for trips during the summer increases significantly in the afternoon and evening hours, especially on weekends, with a peak demands of up to 300. In contrast, there is relatively low demand during the morning rush hour. During spring and winter, however, the demand is lower during the evening rush hours and higher in the morning or afternoon, particularly on weekdays, with demand reaching up to 250. The data demonstrate that Bird's customers use the services primarily for leisure purposes, as demand consistently peaks during the evening rush hour or evening hours, in each season. Figure 5 shows a heatmap visualization for user demand. We can easily notice from the maps that the majority of the frequented areas are touristic or commercial.

(a) Heatmap visualization for starting Bird positions

(b) Heatmap visualization for starting Bird positions zoomed

Fig. 5. Heatmap visualization for Bird demand density

We can notice, from Figs. 3 and 5, that the area's type and period have a great impact on user demand. However, regarding the imbalance problem, it is not sufficient to determine the exact ideal locations to place the fleets dynamically according to the user's needs and enhance user satisfaction and service. Recent studies have demonstrated that using advanced prediction techniques, such as machine learning, can help predict the user demand for an area or a station. These predictions can be based on temporal criteria, such as specific days or time periods of the week [12,18,41]. Given also that weather variables have a significant impact on the use of micro-mobility modes [21,38]; it enables more accuracy in the prediction of user demand by taking into consideration a variety of variable factors like temperature, humidity level or wind speed.

In consequence, we can say that the use of real trips, that have been recorded over time, can effectively help increase the availability of fleets in areas where high future demand is predicted; this helps to reduce the amount of time that users must spend searching for a fleet. This forecast enables operators to properly assess their demand and can provide additional virtual stations in popular regions during specific times, like the summertime, close to tourist areas. By enhancing the user experience, these techniques help operators boost their revenue and improve their services.

Additionally, the user demand prediction tool can improve various aspects, such as pricing strategies and offers, during peak demand periods. It can also improve safety and reduce collisions in areas predicted to be in high demand, or decrease the cost of maintaining devices and replacing batteries. This can be achieved by planning collection operations during times when there is little demand.

5 Conclusion

Shared micro-mobility services face numerous challenges that can negatively impact user satisfaction and company revenue. These challenges include system imbalance, high maintenance costs, infrastructure problems, and safety concerns. To overcome these challenges, machine learning techniques, analytical systems, and decision support systems have been proposed as solutions. These approaches rely on the collected data from shared micro-mobility services, and it has been demonstrated their significance as a crucial element in enhancing service usage. In this study, we analyzed a real-world dataset of recorded trips in Bordeaux, France. The goal was to explore how to leverage this data to improve fleet availability and service quality. By identifying patterns and insights within this data, we can make informed decisions and implement targeted strategies to create a better experience for users and drive greater revenue for companies [27].

References

1. Abduljabbar, R.L., Liyanage, S., Dia, H.: The role of micro-mobility in shaping sustainable cities: a systematic literature review. Transp. Res. Part D: Transp. Environ. **92**, 102734 (2021)
2. Askarzadeh, T., Bridgelall, R.: Micromobility station placement optimization for a rural setting. J. Adv. Transp. **2021**, 1–10 (2021)
3. Bird: Accessed 1 Feb 2023 https://www.bird.co/

4. Bozzi, A.D., Aguilera, A.: Shared e-scooters: a review of uses, health and environmental impacts, and policy implications of a new micro-mobility service. Sustainability **13**(16), 8676 (2021)
5. Cameron Booth, L., Mayrany, M.: IoT penetration testing: Hacking an electric scooter (2019)
6. Chicco, A., Diana, M.: Understanding micro-mobility usage patterns: a preliminary comparison between dockless bike sharing and e-scooters in the city of turin (italy). Transp. Res. Procedia **62**, 459–466 (2022)
7. Feng, C., Jiao, J., Wang, H.: Estimating e-scooter traffic flow using big data to support planning for micromobility. J. Urban Technol. **29**(2), 139–157 (2022)
8. Feng, Y.: Mobile location data analytics, privacy, and security (2020)
9. Fistola, R., Gallo, M., La Rocca, R.A.: Micro-mobility in the "virucity". The effectiveness of e-scooter sharing. Transp. Res. Proc. **60**, 464–471 (2022)
10. Folco, P., Gauvin, L., Tizzoni, M., Szell, M.: Data-driven micromobility network planning for demand and safety. Environment and Planning B: Urban Analytics and City Science, p. 23998083221135611 (2022)
11. Fong, J., McDermott, P., Lucchi, M.: Micro-mobility, e-scooters and implications for higher education. Washington, DC, USA, UPCEA Center for Research and Strategy (2019)
12. Ham, S.W., Cho, J.H., Park, S., Kim, D.K.: Spatiotemporal demand prediction model for e-scooter sharing services with latent feature and deep learning. Transp. Res. Rec. **2675**(11), 34–43 (2021)
13. Hilgert, J.N., Lambertz, M., Hakoupian, A., Mateyna, A.M.: A forensic analysis of micromobility solutions. Forensic Sci. Int. Digit. Invest. **38**, 301137 (2021)
14. Kim, S., Choo, S., Lee, G., Kim, S.: Predicting demand for shared e-scooter using community structure and deep learning method. Sustainability **14**(5), 2564 (2022)
15. Kim, T.S., Lee, W.K., Sohn, S.Y.: Graph convolutional network approach applied to predict hourly bike-sharing demands considering spatial, temporal, and global effects. PLoS ONE **14**(9), e0220782 (2019)
16. Li, Y., Zheng, Y., Yang, Q.: Dynamic bike reposition: a spatio-temporal reinforcement learning approach. In: Proceedings of the 24th ACM SIGKDD International Conference on Knowledge Discovery & Data Mining, pp. 1724–1733 (2018)
17. Lime. Accessed 15 Jan 2023. https://www.li.me/
18. Lin, L., He, Z., Peeta, S.: Predicting station-level hourly demand in a large-scale bike-sharing network: a graph convolutional neural network approach. Transp. Res. Part C: Emerg. Technol. **97**, 258–276 (2018)
19. Marques, D.L., Coelho, M.C.: A literature review of emerging research needs for micromobility-integration through a life cycle thinking approach. Future Transp. **2**(1), 135–164 (2022)
20. Medina-Molina, C., Pérez-Macías, N., Gismera-Tierno, L.: The multi-level perspective and micromobility services. J. Innovation Knowl. **7**(2), 100183 (2022)
21. Milakis, D., Gedhardt, L., Ehebrecht, D., Lenz, B.: Is Micro-mobility Sustainable? An Overview of Implications for Accessibility, Air Pollution, Safety, Physical Activity and Subjective Wellbeing. Handbook of Sustainable Transport, pp. 180–189 (2020)
22. Moralioğlu, B., Cenani, Ş, Çağdaş, G.: A decision support system for placing shared e-scooters: a case study for Istanbul. J. Comput. Des. **2**(2), 127–148 (2021)
23. Pan, L., Cai, Q., Fang, Z., Tang, P., Huang, L.: A deep reinforcement learning framework for rebalancing dockless bike sharing systems. In: Proceedings of the AAAI Conference on Artificial Intelligence, vol. 33, pp. 1393–1400 (2019)

24. Pérez-Zuriaga, A.M., Llopis-Castelló, D., Just-Martínez, V., Fonseca-Cabrera, A.S., Alonso-Troyano, C., García, A.: Implementation of a low-cost data acquisition system on an e-scooter for micromobility research. Sensors **22**(21), 8215 (2022)
25. Phithakkitnukooon, S., Patanukhom, K., Demissie, M.G.: Predicting spatiotemporal demand of dockless e-scooter sharing services with a masked fully convolutional network. ISPRS Int. J. Geo Inf. **10**(11), 773 (2021)
26. Prencipe, L.P., Colovic, A., De Bartolomeo, S., Caggiani, L., Ottomanelli, M.: An efficiency indicator for micromobility safety assessment. In: 2022 IEEE International Conference on Environment and Electrical Engineering and 2022 IEEE Industrial and Commercial Power Systems Europe (EEEIC/I&CPS Europe), pp. 1–6. IEEE (2022)
27. Rania, S., Zeineb, E.K., Imen, J., Mohamed, M.: Free-floating micro-mobility smart redistribution using spatio-temporal demand forecasting. In: Accepted for publication in 14th IEEE Vehicular Networking Conference (VNC). IEEE (2023). In press
28. Sanchez-Iborra, R., Bernal-Escobedo, L., Santa, J.: Eco-efficient mobility in smart city scenarios. Sustainability **12**(20), 8443 (2020)
29. Santa, J., Sanchez-Iborra, R., Rodriguez-Rey, P., Bernal-Escobedo, L., Skarmeta, A.F.: Lpwan-based vehicular monitoring platform with a generic IP network interface. Sensors **19**(2), 264 (2019)
30. Shin, S., Choo, S.: Influence of built environment on micromobility-pedestrian accidents. Sustainability **15**(1), 582 (2022)
31. Spin. Accessed 30 Feb 2023. https://www.spin.app/
32. Turoń, K., Czech, P., Tóth, J.: Safety and security aspects in shared mobility systems. Zeszyty Naukowe, Transport/Politechnika Śląska (2019)
33. Vinayaga-Sureshkanth, N., Wijewickrama, R., Maiti, A., Jadliwala, M.: Security and privacy challenges in upcoming intelligent urban micromobility transportation systems. In: Proceedings of the Second ACM Workshop on Automotive and Aerial Vehicle Security, pp. 31–35 (2020)
34. Voi. Accessed 15 Feb 2023. https://www.voi.com/
35. Wanganoo, L., Shukla, V., Mohan, V.: Intelligent micro-mobility e-scooter: revolutionizing urban transport. Trust-Based Commun. Syst. Internet Things Appl. 267–290 (2022)
36. Watts, M., Brunger, J., Shires, K.: Do European data protection laws apply to the collection of WiFi network data for use in geolocation look-up services? Int. Data Privacy Law **1**(3), 149–160 (2011)
37. Xu, M., Di, Y., Zhu, Z., Yang, H., Chen, X.: Designing van-based mobile battery swapping and rebalancing services for dockless ebike-sharing systems based on the dueling double deep Q-network. Transp. Res. Part C: Emerging Technol. **138**, 103620 (2022)
38. Zhang, C., Dong, M., Luan, T.H., Ota, K.: Battery maintenance of pedelec sharing system: big data based usage prediction and replenishment scheduling. IEEE Trans. Netw. Sci. Eng. **7**(1), 127–138 (2019)
39. Zhang, W., Niu, X., Zhang, G., Tian, L.: Dynamic rebalancing of the free-floating bike-sharing system. Sustainability **14**(20), 13521 (2022)
40. Zhang, Z., Tan, L., Jiang, W.: Free-floating bike-sharing demand prediction with deep learning. Int. J. Mach. Learn. Comput. **12**(2) (2022)
41. Zhou, P., Wang, C., Yang, Y., Wei, X.: E-sharing: data-driven online optimization of parking location placement for dockless electric bike sharing. In: 2020 IEEE 40th International Conference on Distributed Computing Systems (ICDCS), pp. 474–484. IEEE (2020)

Cyber Safety and Security of Intelligent Transportation Systems

Enhancing Autonomous System Security: A Formal Framework for Assessing and Strengthening Autonomous Vehicle Defenses

Samir Ouchani$^{(\boxtimes)}$, Souhila Badra Guendouzi , and Mohamed Amine Boudouaia

CESI LINEACT, Aix-en-Provence, France
{souchani,bguendouzi,aboudouaia}@cesi.fr

Abstract. In recent years, there has been growing concern among experts regarding the risks of hacking autonomous vehicles. As these vehicles become increasingly complex, the number of potential vulnerabilities and challenges associated with securing them also rises. This paper presents a model checking-based framework that utilizes a predefined set of attacks and countermeasures, which are then used to assess the security robustness of the model. First, we formalize a cyber-physical system using Unified Modeling Language (UML) class and activity diagrams. Subsequently, we employ UML to develop a metalanguage for autonomous vehicle systems, cyberattacks, and cybersecurity countermeasures. The framework instantiates domain-specific application diagrams for autonomous vehicles, identifies existing attack surfaces, and generates potential attacks that could exploit detected vulnerabilities or weaknesses. Furthermore, the proposed framework generates appropriate Java code for integrating countermeasures, attacks, and smart vehicle models. To demonstrate the effectiveness of the proposed solution, we model, analyze, harden, and evaluate our framework using a real-world use case. This research aims to contribute to the ongoing efforts to improve the security of autonomous vehicles and mitigate the risks associated with hacking and other cyber threats. By applying the framework presented in this paper, the goal is to promote a more secure development and implementation of autonomous vehicle systems.

Keywords: Cyber Security · Domain Specific Language · Autonomous Vehicles · Threat behavior · Attack Graphs, Counter Measures · UML · JAVA

1 Introduction

The introduction of autonomous vehicles on our roads presents a new set of cybersecurity challenges, as hackers may be able to remotely access and infiltrate on-board systems and networks. These vehicles, with their interconnected components and reliance on digital infrastructure, create a complex environment that is potentially susceptible to various types of cyberattacks. Addressing these security concerns requires tackling two key challenges in the development of secure autonomous vehicles [23].

The first challenge involves early identification of vulnerabilities and weaknesses during the development stage [25]. By proactively uncovering potential security flaws,

I. Jemili et al. (Eds.): DiCES-N 2023, CCIS 2041, pp. 59–82, 2024.
https://doi.org/10.1007/978-3-031-52823-1_4

developers can implement necessary countermeasures to mitigate risks before vehicles are deployed on public roads. This requires a comprehensive understanding of the vehicle's architecture, communication protocols, and software systems, as well as the ability to anticipate potential threats and attack vectors. The second challenge is related to efficiently assessing and quantifying the precise degree of vulnerability of an existing system when exposed to known attacks. This process is crucial for determining the effectiveness of implemented security measures and identifying any remaining gaps that may be exploited by hackers [16]. To achieve this, robust security assessment methodologies and tools must be developed and applied, such as penetration testing, vulnerability scanning, and threat modeling.

Addressing the first challenge necessitates verifying whether a model of the system satisfies a set of relevant security properties. This verification is performed in the presence of an attacker, typically a Dolev Yao adversary [6], possessing significant power to control all the system's communication channels and interfere with its functionality. This analysis technique is known as *model checking* [3]. Model checking has been successfully applied to uncover insidious attacks and anomalies in risk analysis and security assessment for model-based systems [30]. However, although efficiently implemented in specific cases [4], the worst-case time complexity of model checking is exponential in the size of the system's ($|S|$) and the property's ($|P|$) models, i.e., $O(2^{(|S|+|P|)})$. Consequently, large systems may be impractical for this type of analysis. In contrast, addressing the second challenge involves adopting a more pragmatic approach. By considering only documented attacks, the process involves estimating the system's degree of vulnerability by examining its *attack surfaces* [17]. An attack surface can be roughly defined as the set of externally accessible system actions and the system resources that can be modified through those actions. The more extensive the attack surface, the more vulnerable the system can be.

Detecting attack surfaces requires inspecting a system's model and determining if known attacks can reach the system's core procedures via the exposed actions. The literature offers various ways to describe attacks, including attack trees [18], attack graphs [27], and network attack graphs [28]. Such models are utilized by numerous organizations that have a special interest in collecting, describing, and classifying attack patterns. This paper focuses on addressing the second challenge by proposing a formal framework for *automatically* detecting attack surfaces in systems modeled using UML [21], a general-purpose, graphical modeling language designed for specifying, designing, and verifying complex hardware and software systems, as well as organizational and procedural workflows. The UML 2.0-based formalism has become the *de facto* standard in software and systems modeling, making it a pragmatic choice to ensure compliance with current engineering practices.

UML covers various aspects of a system's modeling, particularly its structure and behavior, with its extended profiles MARTE and SysML. Specifically, *class and activity diagrams*, which this work adopts, can express both qualitative and quantitative elements of a system's behavior at various levels of abstraction [10]. A strong system [20] is one in which the cost of an attack is greater than the potential gain to the attacker. Conversely, a weak system is one where the cost of an attack is less than the potential gain. The cost of an attack should take into account not only money but also time to recovery and potential punishment for criminal activities.

To summarize, addressing the cybersecurity challenges in autonomous vehicles requires focusing on two key aspects: early identification of vulnerabilities during the development stage and efficient assessment of existing systems' vulnerability when exposed to known attacks. By employing a combination of model checking and attack surface analysis, developers can better understand and mitigate risks associated with autonomous vehicles. Utilizing UML for system modeling provides a practical and widely-accepted approach for detecting attack surfaces and ensuring compliance with current engineering practices. By taking these steps, the security of autonomous vehicles can be significantly improved, ultimately leading to safer and more reliable transportation systems.

This paper presents an innovative framework for detecting and mitigating attacks in autonomous vehicle systems. By leveraging a model checker-based approach, the framework automatically identifies potential threats and generates secure implementation solutions. The framework starts by creating a meta-model specific to autonomous vehicles and their associated security challenges. This meta-model serves as a blueprint for the system being analyzed, and is modeled using classes and activity diagrams.

Once the input system is modeled, the framework uses attack templates to generate potential attacks on the system's attack surfaces. These attacks are then combined with the instantiated model and appropriate countermeasures to produce a secure implementation. The end result is a transformed autonomous vehicle system, implemented in Java, that is secure and resilient against potential attacks. A visual representation of the framework is shown in Fig. 1. This framework provides a comprehensive solution for ensuring the security of autonomous vehicle systems and mitigating the risks associated with them.

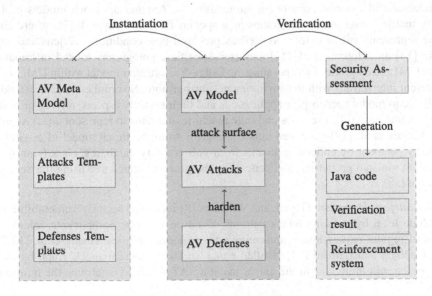

Fig. 1. Secure Autonomous Vehicles Systems.

The remainder of this paper is organized as follows. Section 2 provides a comprehensive review of the existing related work in the field of autonomous vehicle security. In Sect. 3, the necessary background information is formally presented to provide context for the proposed framework. Section 4 introduces the concept of the threat meta-model, specifically designed for autonomous vehicle systems. This section also delves into the details of attack generation and composition. The security assessment of autonomous vehicle systems is presented in Sect. 6. This section demonstrates how the proposed framework can be used to evaluate the security of these systems. The implementation of secure systems is covered in Sect. 7. This section provides insight into how the proposed framework can be used to transform autonomous vehicle systems into secure and resilient systems. The experimental results of the proposed framework are described in Sect. 8. This section provides empirical evidence for the effectiveness of the framework. Finally, Sect. 9 concludes the paper and highlights potential avenues for future research. This section also provides a summary of the key contributions of the paper and the impact of the proposed framework on the field of autonomous vehicle security.

2   Related Work

In this section, we provide an overview of the current initiatives and research efforts related to system attack modeling, attack detection, countermeasures, and their application in the context of autonomous vehicles.

Attack Modeling. A risk-based approach [22] has been proposed to create modular attack trees for each component in the system [9]. These trees are specified as parametric constraints, allowing for the quantification of security breach probabilities due to internal and external component vulnerabilities. Another approach models probability metrics based on attack graphs as a special Bayesian network [7], where each node represents vulnerabilities as well as pre- and post-conditions. Jürjens and Shabalin [14] and Houmb et al. [11] extracted specific cryptography-related information from UMLsec diagrams, incorporating the Dolev-Yao attacker model within UMLsec to represent interactions with the environment. Furthermore, Siveroni et al. [29] extended UMLsec to model peer-to-peer applications and their security aspects, relying on abuse cases defined as UML use cases and state machine diagrams to represent attack scenarios. Morais et al. [19] generated attack scenarios from the threat model of a wireless security protocol by collecting attacks from vulnerability databases, classifying them based on violated properties, and generating the protocol attack tree using the Securel-Tree tool.

Attack Surface Detection. Gegick and Williams [8] identified security vulnerabilities at the code level by tailoring attack patterns based on software components, taking the form of regular expressions representing generic vulnerabilities. Huang et al. [12, 24] and Ouchani and Lenzini [24] distilled attack surfaces from an attack graph by identifying the minimum cost in the graph, using a SAT solver to determine the minimum effort required for an attacker to compromise critical system assets. Vijayakumar et al. [31] developed a runtime analysis-based approach to compute attack surfaces by locating system adversaries and determining which program entry points provide access to adversary-controlled objects, using the system's access control policy to differentiate between adversary-controlled and trusted data. Kantola et al. [15] identified communication attack surfaces by considering intent-based attacks on applications lacking common signature-level permissions, where any component of the correct type with a matching intent filter can intercept the intent, with the potential attacks enabled by such unauthorized intent receipt depending on the intent type. Checkoway et al. [2] systematically analyzed the external attack surface of modern automobile systems, synthesizing the set of possible external attack vectors as a function of the attacker's ability to deliver malicious input via specific modalities and characterizing the attack surface exposed in current automobiles through their set of channels.

Securing Autonomous Vehicles. Joy and Gerla [13] proposed an architecture to guarantee location privacy for mobile users, developing system epochs, a labeled transition-based threat model, and a query measuring location sensitivity. Cui et al. [5] integrated a six-step method to analyze safety and security in compliance with ISO standards 26262 and SAE J3061. Plosz and Varga [26] demonstrated the relationship between threats, attacks, vulnerabilities, and their impacts on autonomous vehicles. Ayub et al. [1] designed an autonomous vehicle to secure sensitive areas from suspicious activities, relying on self-governing navigation and recursive path planning.

By examining these various research efforts, we can gain valuable insights into the current state of attack modeling, detection, and countermeasures for autonomous vehicles. This knowledge will be crucial in the development of more secure and reliable systems, capable of withstanding increasingly sophisticated cyber threats.

3 Systems Modeling Language

In this section, we introduce the modeling diagrams, both structural and behavioral, that form the basis for specifying our security meta language. These diagrams facilitate the representation and analysis of system components and their interactions, enabling the development of a robust security meta language for effective security analysis.

3.1 Structural Models

Any language should provide a semantic foundation for modeling a system's structure and behavior. As a standard graphical language, UML offers mechanisms to represent class members, such as attributes and methods, along with additional information about them. The visibility of attributes or methods can be denoted as follows: $+$ for public, $-$ for private, # for protected, and $\sim$ for package visibility.

- $+$ Public: The attribute or method is accessible from any class within the system.
- $-$ Private: The attribute or method is accessible only within the class it is defined.
- # Protected: The attribute or method is accessible within the class itself and any subclasses or classes within the same package.

- ~ Package: The attribute or method is accessible to classes within the same package, but not to classes outside the package.

By utilizing these visibility symbols in UML, we can effectively model the accessibility and encapsulation of class members in a system's structure and behavior, which is crucial for understanding the security properties of the system.

Further, UML defines various relationships between classes:

- *Dependency*: A semantic connection between dependent and independent model elements. Dependency is denoted by a dashed arrow.
- *Association*: Represents a relationship between instances of classes. Association can be bi-directional, uni-directional, an aggregation (including composition aggregation), or reflexive. Association is denoted by a solid line connecting two classes.
- *Aggregation*: Occurs when a class is a collection or container of other classes. It represents a "whole-part" relationship, but the parts can exist independently of the whole. Aggregation is denoted by a diamond shape at the end of an association line.
- *Composition*: A relationship that represents a stronger "whole-part" relationship where the parts cannot exist independently of the whole. Composition is denoted by a filled diamond shape at the end of an association line.
- *Generalization*: Indicates that one of the two related classes (the subclass) is considered to be a specialized form of the other (the superclass), and the superclass is considered a generalization of the subclass. Generalization is denoted by a hollow triangle at the end of a solid line.
- *Dependency*: A relationship where a class depends on another if the independent class is a parameter variable or local variable of a method of the dependent class. Dependency is denoted by a dashed arrow.

A formal structure of UML diagrams is given in Definition 1.

Definition 1 (Class Diagram). *A class diagram is a tuple* $\mathcal{C} = (C, T, R)$, *where:*

1. C *is a finite set of classes, whereas* $c \in C$ *is a tuple* $\langle A, B \rangle$ *of typed attributes* A *and behaviors* B.
2. $T = \{d, a, s, c, g\}$ *defines the type of a class relations (dependency, aggregation, association, composition, and generalization).*
3. $R : C \times C \rightarrow Ar \times T \times Ar$ *returns the kind of relations between classes and* Ar *defines the multiplicity enumeratison.*

3.2   Behavioral Models

Activity diagrams are UML formalism that focus on a system's behavior. Activity diagrams are graphs: their vertices stand for activities (called *activity nodes*) and their edges stand for connections among activities (called *activity edges*) that define objects/-data flow or control flows. In particular, an activity node ($a \rightarrowtail \mathcal{N}$)can be of the following types:

- *An activity invocation element*: It sends ($a!v \rightarrowtail \mathcal{N}$) or receives ($a?v \rightarrowtail \mathcal{N}$) signals or objects, or it calls an operation or calls a behavior ($a \uparrow A \rightarrowtail \mathcal{N}$).

– A *control flow element*: It defines the initial ($\iota \rightarrowtail \mathcal{N}$)and the final flow of the diagram ($\odot$), or the final flow of a path ($\otimes$), or a decision nodes ($D(\mathcal{A}, p, g, \mathcal{N}, \mathcal{N})$,). It can be a fork ($F(\mathcal{N}_1, \mathcal{N}_2)$), a merge ($M(x) \rightarrowtail \mathcal{N}$) or a join node ($J(x) \rightarrowtail \mathcal{N}$).

An activity edge can be of the following types:

– A *control flow element*: This element represents the execution path through the activity diagram. Incoming edges, which lead to a node from other nodes, are called *input edges*; outgoing edges, which originate from a node and lead to other nodes, are referred to as *output edges*. Understanding the flow of control through these input and output edges is crucial for accurately modeling a system's behavior and identifying potential security vulnerabilities.
– An *object flow element*: This element represents the flow of objects between activity nodes in the activity diagram. Incoming edges are called *input tokens*; outgoing edges are referred to as *output tokens*.

Branching in activity diagrams is modeled using *decision nodes* and *merge nodes*. A decision node specifies a choice between different possible paths. The direction to take depends on the evaluation of a boolean guard, if the decision is boolean. Alternatively, it depends on a probability distribution if the decision is probabilistic. A merge node specifies a point from where different incoming control paths start following the same path.

Concurrency and synchronization are modeled with *fork nodes* and *join nodes*. A fork node indicates the beginning of multiple parallel control threads. In UML 2.0, fork nodes model unrestricted parallelism: thus, a token evolves asynchronously according to an interleaving semantics. A join node allows multiple parallel control threads to synchronize and rejoin (Fig. 2).

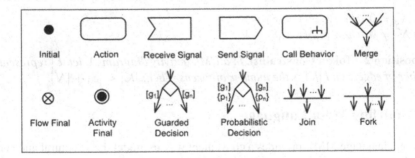

Fig. 2. Activity Diagram Constructs

When an activity diagram is invoked, its initial node activates. It is customary to assume that the initial node activates by possessing a token. A node activates, and thus takes the token, only if the preceding node deactivates and if the condition guarding the node's incoming edge is satisfied. During execution, the action or decision node that has an associated call behavior can consume its input token and invoke its specified behavior. UML supports two types of invocations: synchronous and asynchronous. In the asynchronous invocation, the execution of the invoked behavior proceeds without any further dependency on the execution of the activity that invokes it. In the synchronous invocation, the execution of the calling artifact is blocked until it receives a reply token from the invoked behavior. In a decision node that has more than one path enabled, the choice of which behavior to activate is done non-deterministically.

Definition 2. *A UML activity diagram is a directed graph $G = (N, E)$, where N is the set of activity nodes and E is the set of activity edges. The activity nodes can be of different types, including action nodes, initial nodes, decision nodes, merge nodes, fork nodes, and join nodes. The activity edges connect these nodes and can be of two types: control flow elements and object flow elements.*

Definition 3 (UML Activity Diagram). *A UML activity diagram is a tuple $\mathcal{A} = (\bullet, fin, \mathcal{N}, \mathcal{E}, \mathcal{K}, Prob, Tok)$, where:*

1. *$\bullet$ is the initial node,*
2. *$fin = \{\odot, \otimes\}$ is the set of final nodes,*
3. *$\mathcal{N} = \mathcal{N}_1 \cup \mathcal{N}_2 \cup \mathcal{N}_3$ is a finite set of activity nodes, where $\mathcal{N}_1$, $\mathcal{N}_2$, and $\mathcal{N}_3$ are activity invocation, object and control nodes, respectively.*
4. *$\mathcal{E}$ is a finite set of activity edges,*
5. *$\mathcal{K}$ is a finite set of tokens,*
6. *$Prob : (\{\bullet\} \cup \mathcal{N}) \times \mathcal{E} \to Dist(\mathcal{N} \cup fin)$ is a probabilistic transition function that assigns for each node a discrete probability distribution $\mu \in Dist(\mathcal{N} \cup fin)$,*
7. *$Tok : \mathcal{N} \cup \mathcal{E} \to \mathcal{K}$ is a function that assigns for each node or edge one token.*

Proposition 1 (Structure Constraint). *For a UML activity diagram $\mathcal{A}$, let $|\mathcal{E}|$ be the number of edges, and $|\mathcal{N}| = |\mathcal{N}_1| + |\mathcal{N}_2| + |\mathcal{N}_3|$ is the number of nodes. We have:*

1. *If $\mathcal{N}_3 = \emptyset$, then : $|\mathcal{N}| = |\mathcal{E}| - 1$*
2. *If $\mathcal{N}_3 \neq \emptyset$, then : $|\mathcal{N}| < |\mathcal{E}| - 1$*

Proposition 2 (Token Constraint). *In a UML activity diagram $\mathcal{A}$, let $|\mathcal{E}|$ represent the number of edges, and $|\mathcal{K}|$ is the number of tokens. Then: $|\mathcal{K}| < |\mathcal{E}| + |\mathcal{N}|$.*

4 Modeling Meta Language

The meta language MML provides a convenient way to model the structural and behavioral design of an autonomous vehicle (AV), its potential threats and attacks, and the available countermeasures. MML builds upon the foundation of UML, extending its capabilities to better represent security aspects of a system.

Definition 4. *The Meta Modeling Language (MML) is an extension of UML designed for modeling the security aspects of a system, including threats, attacks, and countermeasures. MML combines the structural and behavioral modeling capabilities of UML with additional constructs that facilitate the representation of security-related elements and their relationships.*

By incorporating MML into the design process of an AV, engineers can gain a deeper understanding of the system's potential vulnerabilities and the effectiveness of various countermeasures. MML makes it easier to identify and mitigate security risks, ensuring a more robust and secure design for autonomous vehicles.

4.1 AV Model

Figure 3 depicts the class diagram of the meta-model for an autonomous vehicle (AV). In an AV, an entity can be an object, a device, and/or a social actor. The class protocol ensures the communication between the server, device, and objects. An object can be physical (e.g., sensor) or digital (e.g., message, data) with varying degrees of specificity and capabilities. A device is an object with a system (e.g., PC, smartphone, etc.) and can make decisions according to its behavior. Social actors can vary depending on the model's system, but typically interact with others, manipulate objects, and access resources. The AV meta-model provides a way to represent the various components of an autonomous vehicle and their relationships. By incorporating this meta-model into the design process, engineers can more easily identify potential vulnerabilities and develop appropriate countermeasures. Additionally, the AV meta-model can facilitate communication between different stakeholders, such as engineers and security analysts, by providing a common language for discussing the design and security aspects of an AV.

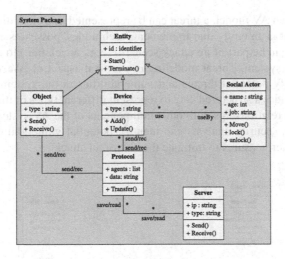

Fig. 3. A AV Meta-Model.

4.2 AV Environment

Figure 4 shows the class diagram of the meta-model for an autonomous vehicle (AV) environment. An environment can be a human body, a natural species, or a physical space that hosts the system and interacts with its components. In the context of AVs, the environment plays a crucial role in determining the system's behavior and its interaction with external entities. For example, the weather, traffic conditions, and road infrastructure can affect an AV's decision-making process and overall performance. Additionally, the presence of other vehicles, pedestrians, and animals in the environment can pose safety challenges for the AV.

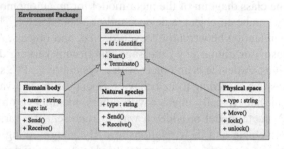

Fig. 4. A AV environment Meta-Model.

4.3   Threat Model

In the context of an AV model, a threat can be represented as a class diagram, as shown in Fig. 5. A threat is an entity that implements techniques, possesses certain skills and knowledge, and can be part of an attack scenario (e.g., attack tree) to exploit a vulnerability in the AV system. Threat modeling is a critical aspect of AV security analysis, as it helps identify potential threats and vulnerabilities in the system. The AV threat meta-model provides a structured way to represent different types of threats, their capabilities, and their relationships with other components of the AV system. By analyzing the threat model, security analysts can identify potential vulnerabilities and develop appropriate countermeasures to mitigate the risk of an attack.

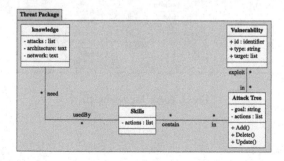

Fig. 5. Threat Model.

4.4 Counter Measure Model

A countermeasure is a defense mechanism that is designed to protect a system against potential attacks. In the context of AV security, countermeasures can be implemented to mitigate vulnerabilities that may be exploited by an attacker. Figure 6 shows the class diagram of the metamodel for countermeasures in an AV system.

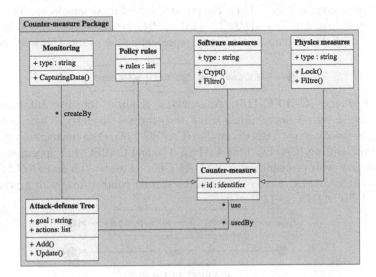

Fig. 6. Counter-Measure Model.

As shown in the diagram, a countermeasure can be associated with a set of vulnerabilities that it is designed to mitigate. Examples of countermeasures include monitoring, security policy rules, software measures (such as encryption and access controls), and physical measures (such as secure storage and biometric authentication).

4.5 Threat Behaviors

The standard schema for describing attack patterns is the Common Attack Patterns Enumeration and Classification (CAPEC) developed by the software assurance strategic initiative. We specifically considered two categories of attacks to be relevant for our work: *software attacks* (CAPEC-513) and *communications attacks* (CAPEC-512). The software attacks category includes twenty-five attacks, such as Brute Force (CAPEC-112) and Authentication Abuse (CAPEC-114). Due to space limitations, we cannot list all the attacks in this category, but they can be found in the CAPEC taxonomy. The communications attack category includes two attacks: Interception (CAPEC-117) and Protocol Manipulation (CAPEC-272). These attacks are important to consider when assessing the security of autonomous vehicles, as they can have significant impacts on the system's functionality and safety. By identifying and analyzing these attacks, we can better understand the potential vulnerabilities of the system and develop appropriate countermeasures to mitigate them. We present models for a chosen set of technical attacks, as follows.

- **Spoofing (CAPEC-156):** An attacker impersonates a trusted source by crafting a fake message that mimics an authorized one. Recipients of these messages may be deceived into responding or processing the misleading message. Spoofing can involve altering the message's content (CAPEC-148) or falsifying the message's sender or receiver (CAPEC-151). The probabilities of these attacks are illustrated in the figure below, with $P(CAPEC-148) = P(CAPEC-151) = 0.8$. We assign a value of 0.8 due to their high severity, representing the average between 60% and 100%.

- **Data Leakage (CAPEC-118):** An attacker acquires sensitive information by exploiting design vulnerabilities using well-formed requests. Three techniques belong to this category: Data excavation (CAPEC-116), Data interception (CAPEC-117), and Sniffing (CAPEC-148). CAPEC-116 and CAPEC-117 appear in the first control flow with probabilities of $P(CAPEC-116) = 0.5$ and $P(CAPEC-117) = 0.5$. CAPEC-148 is shown in the second control flow with a probability value of $P(CAPEC-148) = 0.2$.

CAPEC-117 P=0.2

- **Resource Depletion (CAPEC-119):** An attacker exhausts a resource to the point where the target's functionality is impacted, typically causing the degradation or denial of one or more services. The attacker can achieve their goal through flooding (CAPEC-125), leaking (CAPEC-131) by uploading a malicious file, or allocation (CAPEC-131) by sending a formatted request. The pattern of these attacks is depicted in the following diagram, where n represents the number of requests and m is a number determined by the designer. These attacks are launched with probabilities of $P(CAPEC-125) = 0.8$ and $P(CAPEC-131) = 0.8$.

- **Injection (CAPEC-152):** An attacker manipulates or disrupts a target's behavior by sending specially crafted input data via an interface that processes this data. Various patterns, dependent on the resources, are documented in CAPEC and abstracted to a design level, including SQL (CAPEC-66), email (CAPEC-134), format string (CAPEC-135), LDAP (CAPEC-136), resource injection (CAPEC-240), script injection (CAPEC-242), and command injection (CAPEC-248). These patterns share a common control flow with an 80% probability, as depicted in Fig. 7.

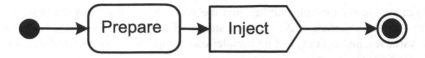

Fig. 7. Control flow for Injection (CAPEC-152)

Fig. 8. Workflow for Exploitation of Authentication (CAPEC-225).

- **Exploitation of Authentication (CAPEC-225):** Attackers exploit vulnerabilities in authentication mechanisms, such as authentication bypass via spoofing (CWE-290), authentication bypass using assumed immutable data (CWE-302), and origin validation error (CWE-346). The sub-category CAPEC-21 focuses on exploiting session variables, resource IDs, and other trusted credentials by taking advantage of software that accepts user input without verifying its authenticity. This attack follows the workflow illustrated in Fig. 8 with an 80% probability.
- **Fuzzing (CAPEC-28):** This attack, inspired by a software testing method, employs a probabilistic technique (CAPEC-223). The attacker submits randomly generated input to the system and monitors it for indications of potential weaknesses. The attack pattern is characterized by the control flow described below, with P(CAPEC-28) = 0.8 and $P_1, P_2, \cdots, P_n$ representing probability values (e.g., uniformly distributed), as demonstrated in Fig. 9.

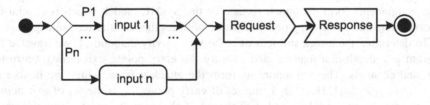

Fig. 9. Control flow for Fuzzing (CAPEC-28).

5 Systems-Attack-Defense Composition

By relying on the developed diagrams, we can instantiate concrete models for a real case by providing specific values for the attributes and methods of the classes in the class diagrams. This allows us to create a concrete system model that can be analyzed for potential security vulnerabilities.

5.1 Attack Surfaces Detection

A system's attack surface is related to its exposed vulnerabilities, which in turn affects an adversary's ability to interfere with and damage the system. The larger the attack surface, the greater the vulnerability, and the more potential attacks the system may suffer. An attack surface is defined as a subset of a system's resources, typically its data, variables, and actions, that an intruder can control and used to interfere with the system's behavior.

Entry and exit points refer to the system's artifacts used to receive and send objects, respectively. A channel connects an attacker to a system, and untrusted data refers to persistent data that can be read (received) or written (sent) by an entry or exit point, respectively. The concept of *untrusted objects* is defined in Definition 5.

Definition 5. *[Untrusted Object] An object v is* untrusted *if it is acquired by an input action or if it depends on an untrusted object. An object v depends on another object w if v is calculated from w.*

Definition 6 formalizes the notion of attack surface in SysML terms:

Definition 6. (Attack Surface). *Let A be a SysML model. An attack surface is a tuple $\omega = \langle N, X, O, Ch \rangle$, where:*

1. *N is the set of entry points of A, which are all artifacts except send artifacts.*
2. *X is the set of exit points of A, which are the send artifacts.*
3. *O is the set of untrusted objects of A.*
4. *$Ch : N \cup X \rightarrow 2^O$ maps entry or exit points to untrusted objects.*

In this definition, N represents the set of entry points of the SysML model, which are all artifacts except send artifacts, while X represents the set of exit points, which are the send artifacts. O is the set of untrusted objects, which are objects that are either acquired by an input action or depend on another untrusted object, as per Definition 5. The function Ch maps each entry or exit point to a set of untrusted objects. Together, these components form the attack surface of the SysML model, which is crucial for understanding and identifying potential vulnerabilities that an attacker can exploit.

To determine the attack surfaces of a SysML activity diagram A, we traverse the diagram in a depth-first manner, and identify the entry points, exit points, untrusted data, and channels. These components form the attack surface, which we denote by $\Omega = (\omega_1, \omega_2, \omega_3, \omega_4)$. Here, ω_1 is the set of entry points, ω_2 is the set of exit points, ω_3 is the set of untrusted data, and ω_4 is the set of channels. By constructing the attack surface in this way, we can identify the specific parts of the system that an attacker can potentially exploit to compromise the security of the system.

5.2   Application-Dependent Attacks Generation

Our objective is to assign appropriate attack templates for each attack surface detected by Algorithm 1 and instantiate them for the system under study. To accomplish this, we propose the function Λ described in Listing 1.1, which assigns at least one attack $k \in \mathbb{K}$ to each attack surface $\omega \in \Omega$. Here, $\mathbb{K}$ is the set of attacks, where each k_i corresponds to a specific CAPEC id: k_1 is CAPEC-148, k_2 is CAPEC-151, k_3 is CAPEC-116, k_4 is CAPEC-117, k_5 is CAPEC-125, k_6 is CAPEC-131, k_7 is CAPEC-148, k_8 is CAPEC-152, k_9 is CAPEC-225, k_{10} is CAPEC-28, and k_{11} is CAPEC-163.

Listing 1.1. Attack-System Composition.

$$\Lambda : \Omega \to 2^{\mathbb{K}}$$

$\Lambda(\omega) = \forall \omega \in \Omega,\ \text{Case}\ (\omega)\ \textbf{of}$

$\quad \iota \mapsto \mathcal{N} \Rightarrow \textbf{in}\ \{k_1, k_6, k_7, k_{11}\} \cup \Lambda(\mathcal{N})\ \textbf{end}$

$\quad a \mapsto \mathcal{N} \Rightarrow \textbf{in}\ \{k_2, k_4\} \cup \Lambda(\mathcal{N})\ \textbf{end}$

$\quad a \uparrow \mathcal{A} \mapsto \mathcal{N} \Rightarrow \textbf{in} \{k_3, k_4, k_{10}, k_{11}\} \cup \Lambda(\mathcal{N}) \cup \Lambda(\mathcal{A})\ \textbf{end}$

$\quad a!v \mapsto \mathcal{N} \Rightarrow \textbf{in}\ \{k_2, k_3, k_4\} \cup \Lambda(\mathcal{N}) \textbf{end}$

$\quad a?v \mapsto \mathcal{N} \Rightarrow \textbf{in}\ \{k_1, k_8, k_{11}\} \cup \Lambda(\mathcal{N})\ \textbf{end}$

$\quad D(\mathcal{A}, p, g, \mathcal{N}_1, \mathcal{N}_2) \Rightarrow \textbf{in}\ \{k_5, k_7, k_9, k_{11}\} \cup \Lambda(\mathcal{N}_1) \cup \Lambda(\mathcal{N}_2) \cup \Lambda(\mathcal{A})\ \textbf{end}$

$\quad M(x, y) \mapsto \mathcal{N} \Rightarrow \textbf{in}\ \{k_5, k_9\} \cup \Lambda(\mathcal{N})\ \textbf{end}$

$\quad F(\mathcal{N}_1, \mathcal{N}_2) \Rightarrow \textbf{in} \{k_5, k_9\} \cup \Lambda(\mathcal{N}_1) \cup \Lambda(\mathcal{N}_2)\ \textbf{end}$

$\quad J(x, y) \mapsto \mathcal{N} \Rightarrow \textbf{in}\ \{k_5, k_9\} \cup \Lambda(\mathcal{N})\ \textbf{end}$

$\quad \textbf{else} \Rightarrow \textbf{in}\ \{\}\ \textbf{end}$

5.3 AV Defense

We propose a set of countermeasures to minimize attack surfaces and counteract attack actions. At this level of AV design, countermeasures can be preventive (e.g., firewall, antivirus) or reactive (e.g., adding security guards) after a successful attack. In this work, we consider the following measures:

- Policy access control: This restricts the use and access to resources. We adopt the role-based access control (RBAC) mechanism to model this defense.
- Encryption: This ensures confidentiality and data integrity. We use symmetric and asymmetric key encryption.
- Intrusion detection: This is a prevention mechanism from known attacks.
- Secure communication: This allows a sensor node running on a system to communicate with an external node running on a different system. Initially, we integrate IPsec using AES-CCM.
- Reputation-based secure routing: This guarantees the continuity of the routing service by selecting trusted neighbor nodes. At this level, we use a signature-based detection method.

6 AV Security Assessment

For the security assessment, we rely on the probabilistic and symbolic model checker PRISM to verify the security requirements expressed in the probabilistic computation tree logic (PCTL). A PRISM program is a composition of a set of *modules* defined as a set of variables and commands. The evaluation of variables defines the state of a module, whereas commands define their transitions. PRISM expresses a probabilistic command as $[\alpha]\ g \to p_1 : u_1 + ... + p_m : u_m$, where p_i is a probability value ($p_i \in]0, 1[$ and $\sum_{i=0}^{m} p_i = 1$), α is a label that names the action α, g is the guard over all variables expressed as a propositional logic formula, and u_i describes the *update* of variables. An update takes the form $(v'_j = val_j) \cdots (v'_k = val_k)$ to assign the value val_i to only a local variable v_i. So, for a given action α, if the guard g is valid, then the update u_i

is enabled with a probability p_i. When $p = 1$, it is a simple command expressed by $[a] \, g \rightarrow u$.

Syntactically, a module named M is delimited by two keywords: the module head "module M", and the module termination "endmodule". Further, we can model costs with reward module R delimited by keywords "rewards R" and "endrewards". A reward module is composed from a *state reward* or a *transition reward*. A state reward associates a cost (reward) of value r to any state satisfying g and it is expressed by $g : r$. A transition reward is specified by $[a] \, g : r$ to express that the transitions labeled a, from states satisfying g, are acquiring the reward of value r.

Finally, for the analysis, we have to generate a PRISM program P proper to the provided formalism. For that, we define the function $\mathcal{T}_P$ that assigns for each node behavior its proper PRISM code fragment that is bounded by 'module node name' and 'endmodule' and the semantic rules of each action is expressed by a PRISM command.

For an automatic assessment of security in AV, we develop $\mathcal{T}_P$ (Listing 1.2) that transforms the structural and behavioral diagrams of a given AV model into a PRISM code. The security requirements are expressed in PCTL as follows.

$$\phi ::= \top \mid ap \mid \phi \wedge \phi \mid \neg \phi \mid P_{\bowtie p}[\psi]$$
$$\psi ::= X\phi \mid \phi U^{\leq k}\phi \mid \phi U\phi$$

where the term "$\top$" means *true*, "ap" is an atomic proposition, $k \in \mathbb{N}$, $p \in [0, 1]$, and $\bowtie \in \{<, \leq, >, \geq\}$. The operator "$\wedge$" represents the *conjunction* and "$\neg$" is the *negation* operator, and P is the probabilistic operator. Also, "X", "$U^{\leq k}$", and "U" are the *next*, the *bounded until*, and the *until* temporal logic operators, respectively.

Listing 1.2. PRISM Code Geneation.

```
T : A → P
T(A) = ∀n ∈ A, L(n = ι) = T, L(n ≠ ι) = ⊥, Case(n) of
ι : ι ↦ N  ⇒  in {[l]l —→ (l' = ⊥)&(L(N)' = T); } ∪ T(N)  end
ι : M(x, y) ↦ N  ⇒  in {[lₓ]lₓ —→ (l'ₓ = ⊥)&(L(N)' = T); }∪{[l_y]l_y —→ (l'_y = ⊥)&(L(N)' = T); } ∪ T(N)end
ι : J(x, y) ↦ N  ⇒in {[l]lₓ ∧ l_y —→ (l'_y = ⊥)&(l'_y = ⊥)&(L(N)' = T); }cupT(N)end
ι : F(N₁, N₂)  ⇒  in {[l]l —→ (l' = ⊥)&(L(N₁)' = T)&(L(N₂)' = T); } ∪ T(N₁) ∪ T(N₂)  end
ι : D(A, p, g, N₁, N₂)⇒Case (p) of ]0, 1[ ⇒in
{[l]l —→ p : (l' = ⊥)&(l'_g = T) + (1 − p) : (l' = ⊥)&(l'_¬g = T); } ∪ {[l_¬g]l_g ∧ ¬g —→ (l'_¬g = ⊥)&(L(N₂)' = T); }
∪{[l_g]l_g ∧ g —→ (l'_g = ⊥)&(L(N₁)' = T); } ∪ T(N₁) ∪ T(N₂)end
Otherwise in {[l]l —→ (l' = ⊥)&(l'_g = T); } ∪ {[l]l —→ (l' = ⊥)&(l'_¬g = T); }
∪{[l_g]l_g ∧ g —→ (l'_g = ⊥)&(L(N₁)' = T); } ∪ {[l_¬g]l_g ∧ ¬g —→ (l'_¬g = ⊥)&(L(N₂)' = T); } ∪ T(N₁) ∪ T(N₂)end
ι : aB ↦ N, Case (B) of↑ A_i ⇒in {[l]l → (l' = ⊥); }
∪{[L(E(A_i))]L(E(A_i)) → (l' = ⊥)&(L(N)' = T); } ∪ T'(A_i);  end
ε  ⇒  in {[l]l —→ (l' = ⊥)&(N' = T); } ∪ T(N')  end
ι : ⊗  ⇒  in [l]l —→ (l' = ⊥);  end
ι : ⊙⇒  in [l]l —→ &_{l∈L}(l' = ⊥);end
```

7   AV Code Generation

This section generates Java code corresponding to the diagrams presented in Sect. 4. The function Λ_c generates the Java code that corresponds to a class diagram, as shown in Listing 1.3.

Listing 1.3. Class diagram to Java Code.

```
Λc : C → J
Λc(c) = ∀c, c1, c2 ∈ C, Case (c) of
c ⇒ in public final class c {}end
p ⇒ in package p.name; end
a ∈ Att(c) ⇒ in public class c { vis(a) type(a) _a;} end
g ∈ c1 × c2 ⇒ in public abstract class c1 {}
public final class c2 extends c1 {} end
r ∈ c1 × c2 ⇒ in public abstract class c1 {}
public final class c2 implements c1 {} end
s ∈ c1 × c2 ⇒ in public final class c1 {private c2 _c1,2;} public final class c2{} end
c ∈ c1 × c2 ⇒ in public final class c1 {private final c2; private c1() {_c2 = new c2();}}
public final class c2 {} end
d ∈ c1 × c2 ⇒ in public final class c1{public use(c2 c2){}}
public final class c2{public void method(){C c;}} public final class C {}
else ⇒ in {} end
```

8 Experimental Results

In this section, we present the specification of an autonomous vehicle (AV) system and its corresponding threat behavior using our MML. We also define the requirement properties for the system. The MML allows us to model the structural and behavioral design of an AV, along with its possible threats and attacks, and the existing countermeasures. By using the MML, we can easily instantiate concrete models for real cases, compose an attack for a concrete system, and reinforce it using predefined countermeasures.

Model's System

In the specification with our MML, the base class is *Vehicle*, which is instantiated from the *Object* class. The methods of the class represent its behavior, and two objects, *Vision* and *Lidar*, are responsible for detecting obstacles, creating a 3D map, and sending it to the *Controller*. The localization system is represented by three classes: *GPS*, which represents the device in the vehicle and is instantiated from the *Device* class; *GSM*, which is a communication protocol instantiated from the *Protocol* class; and *GPS Server*, which represents the station of the GSM network and is also instantiated from the *Protocol* class. Additionally, the driver is represented by the *Driver* class, which is instantiated from the *Social Actor* class and can control the vehicle either manually or through voice commands. The vehicle has a voice detector, which is represented by the *Voice* class and is also instantiated from the *Object* class (Fig. 10).

Attackers Behavior

In the case of the drone attack, the drone is considered as an external attacker that targets the AV's communication system. The attacker can use a laser to interfere with the communication between the AV and the GPS server or other vehicles, which can cause a DDoS attack. The DDoS attack can lead to a denial of service for the AV, and thus affect its ability to perform its tasks and ensure safety.

As for the malware attack, the attacker targets the driver's smartphone, which is considered as a vulnerable entry point to the AV system. By infecting the smartphone

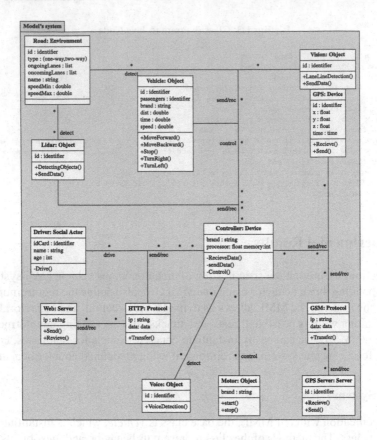

Fig. 10. Model's system of autonomous vehicle.

with malware, the attacker can gain access to the AV system and take control of the vehicle through the smartphone. The attacker can manipulate the AV's behavior and compromise its safety, posing a significant threat to the passengers and other road users.

First Attacker. Figure 12 provides a visual representation of the attacker's model, which is broken down into various components. The first component, the class *KLidar*, represents the attacker's knowledge about the Lidar sensor, such as its communication frequency and other important technical details. This knowledge plays a crucial role in enabling the attacker to target the system effectively.

The second component, the class *VLidar*, represents the vulnerabilities inherent in the Lidar sensor. These vulnerabilities are potential points of weakness that the attacker may exploit in order to disrupt or compromise the sensor's functionality. By understanding these vulnerabilities, the attacker can better plan their attack strategy and maximize the potential for success.

The attacker's skills are represented by the class *Dos Attack*, which signifies that the attacker is primarily capable of carrying out Denial of Service (DoS) attacks. This type of attack aims to overwhelm the target system, rendering it inoperable or significantly degraded in performance. The attacker's specialization in DoS attacks may limit their range of tactics, but it also allows them to focus on honing their skills in this specific area.

The attack process itself is depicted in a separate activity diagram, which is included in Sect. 4.5 and titled *Resource Depletion (CAPEC-119)*. This diagram illustrates the various steps involved in the attack, from initial reconnaissance and probing to the actual execution of the DoS attack. It provides a clear and concise visualization of the attacker's actions, enabling a better understanding of the attacker's methodology and the potential countermeasures that can be employed to mitigate the risk of such an attack (Fig. 11).

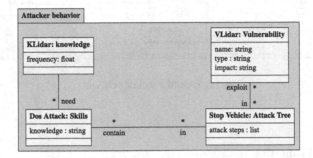

Fig. 11. First attacker behavior.

Second Attacker. Figure 12 illustrates the model of the attacker, focusing on their knowledge, vulnerabilities, and skills related to the network. The class *Network:Knowledge* represents the attacker's understanding of the deployed communication protocols within the network. This knowledge enables the attacker to identify potential weaknesses and areas of opportunity within the network infrastructure, which may be exploited during an attack.

The class *Network:Vulnerability* highlights the vulnerabilities associated with the network protocols in use. These vulnerabilities could stem from design flaws, implementation errors, or misconfigurations, and they serve as potential targets for the attacker. By being aware of these vulnerabilities, the attacker can develop and refine their attack strategies to exploit these weak points effectively.

The attacker's skills are represented by the class *Network:skills*, which indicates their ability to conduct network-related attacks. This could include activities such as eavesdropping, packet manipulation, or network-based Denial of Service (DoS) attacks. The attacker's proficiency in these skills can significantly impact the effectiveness of their attack and the level of damage they can inflict on the target network.

The activity diagram of the CAPEC-156 attack is provided in Sect. 4.5. This diagram outlines the various steps involved in executing the attack, from initial reconnaissance to the actual exploitation of network vulnerabilities. By examining this activity diagram, security professionals can gain a better understanding of the attacker's tactics and techniques, which can then be used to develop more effective defenses and countermeasures against such threats.

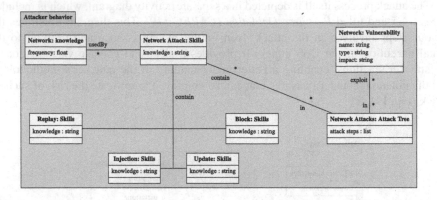

Fig. 12. Second attacker behavior.

Requirement Properties

We have defined three properties to see if the attacker may violate the properties or not.

- The attacker could not stop the car. $P =?[\Box((CurentPosition \neq destinitation) \wedge (Run = \top))]$
- The attacker could not change the destination of the car. $P =?[\Box(destinitation = target)]$
- Could the car know when to stop. $P =?[\Box(Time2Destinitation = EstimedTime)]$

Verification Result

The results, obtained from the verification are summarized in Table 1 where the symbol ✓ means an attack has been found and the symbol ✗ means that the property is safe.

Table 1. The verification results.

Property/Attacker	First Attacker	Second Attacker
Φ_1	✗	✗
Φ_2	✓	✗
Φ_3	✓	✗

The first attacker can violate only Φ_1 because his knowledge and skills are limited, it will go near to the vehicle and send signals with the laser to saturate the channel to cause denial-of-service of the Laser and that will stop the vehicle.

The second attacker can violate all the properties, because he is inside the network and he uses the smartphone of the victim which allows him to control totally the car, he needs only to install the malware on the smartphone by a fishing e-mail.

Reinforcement Recommendation

Figure 13 shows the counter-measure used to monitor and detect abnormal behavior, it adds physical solutions to absorb signals attacks in addition to a secure channel.

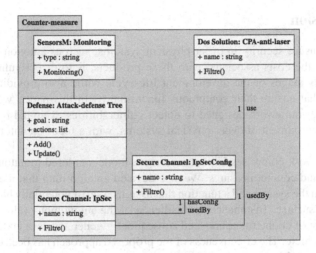

Fig. 13. Counter-Measure.

Secure Vehicle Implementation

Listing 1.4 presents the java code for the class diagram of the vehicle, the attack, and the counter measures.

Listing 1.4. Vehicule-System Java Code.

```
public class Vehicle {
private String id ;...
public void start ();...
public void stop ();...
private Vision _vision ();
private Road _road ();
private Lidar _lidar ();
private Controller _controller ();...    }
```

```
public class Ddos {
private String id;
private String goal;...
private StopVehicle _stopvehicle;
private KLidar _klidar;}
public class DefenseDos {
private String goal;
private action list actions;...
public void add();
public void update();...
private PhysicMeasures _physicmeasure;
private SensorsM _sensorm;}
```

9 Conclusion

One way to ensure security in cyber-physical systems, such as autonomous vehicles, and to reduce the costs associated with these products, is to detect vulnerabilities to attacks at early stages of the development life-cycle while also providing correction mechanisms that ensure their continuous functionality. In this paper, we presented a comprehensive framework designed to detect vulnerabilities exploited by attacks in a specialized environment of cyber-physical systems, with a focus on autonomous vehicles.

Our framework comprises UML-based meta-models tailored to autonomous vehicles, attacks, and countermeasures. We also devised an algorithm that identifies attack surfaces within the system and a function that assigns a set of potentially harmful attacks to each attack surface. To enhance the resilience of the autonomous vehicle, we implemented a range of countermeasures and subsequently generated Java code for a secure autonomous vehicle. The effectiveness of the proposed approach has been demonstrated through a real-world case study involving a smart autonomous vehicle operating in a malicious environment.

In the near future, we plan to expand our research in several directions. Firstly, we aim to apply our framework to various real-world scenarios, broadening the scope of its applicability. Secondly, we aspire to develop a more comprehensive catalog encompassing a wider range of attack types and countermeasures, including those relevant to the supply chain. Lastly, an essential task is to implement and validate the correctness of the proposed approach, ensuring that it delivers the intended outcomes in securing cyber-physical systems like autonomous vehicles.

By addressing these future goals, our research will contribute to the ongoing efforts to safeguard autonomous vehicles and other cyber-physical systems against potential threats, ultimately improving their security, reliability, and overall performance in an increasingly interconnected world.

References

1. Ayub, M.F., Ghawash, F., Shabbir, M.A., Kamran, M., Butt, F.A.: Next generation security and surveillance system using autonomous vehicles. In: 2018 Ubiquitous Positioning,

Indoor Navigation and Location-Based Services (UPINLBS), pp. 1–5 (2018). https://doi.org/10.1109/UPINLBS.2018.8559744
2. Checkoway , S., et al.: Comprehensive experimental analyses of automotive attack surfaces. In Proceedings of the 20th USENIX Conference on Security (SEC 11), pp. 6–6. USENIX Association (2011)
3. Clarke, E.M., Emerson, E.A., Sistla, A.P.: Automated verification of finite state concurrent systems using temporal logic specifications: a practical approach. In: Proceedings of POPL, pp. 117–126 (1983)
4. Clarke, E.M., Klieber, W., Nováček, M., Zuliani, P.: Model checking and the state explosion problem. In: Meyer, B., Nordio, M. (eds.) LASER 2011. LNCS, vol. 7682, pp. 1–30. Springer, Heidelberg (2012). https://doi.org/10.1007/978-3-642-35746-6_1
5. Cui, J., Sabaliauskaite, G., Liew, L.S., Zhou, F., Zhang, B.: Collaborative analysis framework of safety and security for autonomous vehicles. IEEE Access 7, 148672–148683 (2019). ISSN 2169–3536
6. Dolev, D., Yao, A.: On the security of public key protocols. IEEE Trans. Inf. Theory 29(2), 198–208 (1983). ISSN 0018–9448
7. Frigault, M., Wang, L.: Measuring network security using Bayesian network-based attack graphs. In: Proceedings of the 32nd IEEE International Computer Software and Applications Conference (COMPSAC 2008), pp. 698–703 (2008)
8. Gegick, M., Williams, L.: On the design of more secure software-intensive systems by use of attack patterns. Inf. Softw. Technol. 49, 381–397 (2007)
9. Grunske, L., Joyce, D.: Quantitative risk-based security prediction for component-based systems with explicitly modeled attack profiles. J. Syst. Softw. 81, 1327–1345 (2008)
10. Holt, J., Perry, S.: SysML for Systems Engineering. Institution of Engineering and Technology Press, London (2007)
11. Houmb, S.H., Islam, S., Knauss, E., Schneider, K.: Eliciting security requirements and tracing them to design: an integration of common criteria, heuristics, and UMLsec. Requir. Eng. 15, 63–93 (2010). ISSN 0947–3602 ISSN 0947–3602
12. Huang, H., Zhang, S., Ou, X., Prakash, A., Sakallah, K.: Distilling critical attack graph surface iteratively through minimum-cost sat solving. In: ACSAC 2011, pp. 31–40 (2011)
13. Joy, J., Gerla, M.: Internet of vehicles and autonomous connected car - privacy and security issues. In: 2017 26th International Conference on Computer Communication and Networks (ICCCN), pp. 1–9 (2017). https://doi.org/10.1109/ICCCN.2017.8038391
14. Jürjens, J., Shabalin, P.: Automated verification of UMLsec models for security requirements. In: UML 2004, the Unified Modeling Language. LNCS, vol. 2460, pp. 412–425. Springer (2004)
15. Kantola, D., Chin, E., He, W., Wagner, D.: Reducing attack surfaces for intra-application communication in android. In: Proceedings of the 2nd ACM Workshop on Security and Privacy in Smartphones and Mobile Devices (SPSM 12), pp. 69–80. ACM (2012)
16. Khaled, A., Ouchani, S., Tari, Z., Drira, K.: Assessing the severity of smart attacks in industrial cyber-physical systems. ACM Trans. Cyber Phys. Syst., 5(1), 10:1–10:28 (2021). https://doi.org/10.1145/3422369
17. Manadhata, P.K., Wing, J.M.: An attack surface metric. IEEE Trans. on Soft. Eng. 37(3), 371–386 (2011). ISSN 0098–5589
18. Mauw, S., Oostdijk, M.: Foundations of attack trees. In: Won, D.H., Kim, S. (eds.) ICISC 2005. LNCS, vol. 3935, pp. 186–198. Springer, Heidelberg (2006). https://doi.org/10.1007/11734727_17
19. Morais, A., Hwang, I., Cavalli, A., Martins, E.: Generating attack scenarios for the system security validation. Networking Sci. 2(3–4), 69–80 (2013). ISSN 2076–0310
20. OGorman, L.: Comparing passwords, tokens, and biometrics for user authentication. Proc. IEEE 91(12), 2021–2040 (2003)

21. OMG. OMG Systems Modeling Language (OMG SysML) Specification. Object Management Group (2017)
22. Ouchani, S., Mohamed, O.A., Debbabi, M.: A security risk assessment framework for SysML activity diagrams. In: 2013 IEEE 7th International Conference on Software Security and Reliability, pp. 227–236 (2013)
23. Ouchani, S., Khaled, A.: Security assessment and hardening of autonomous vehicles. In: Garcia-Alfaro, J., Leneutre, J., Cuppens, N., Yaich, R. (eds.) CRiSIS 2020. LNCS, vol. 12528, pp. 365–375. Springer, Cham (2021). https://doi.org/10.1007/978-3-030-68887-5_24
24. Ouchani, S., Lenzini, G.: Attacks generation by detecting attack surfaces. Procedia Comput. Sci. **32**, 529–536 (2014). ISSN 1877–0509. The 5th International Conference on Ambient Systems, Networks and Technologies (ANT-2014), the 4th International Conference on Sustainable Energy Information Technology (SEIT-2014)
25. Ouchani, S., Mohamed, O.A., Debbabi, M., Pourzandi, M.: Verification of the correctness in composed UML behavioural diagrams. In: Lee, R., Ormandjieva, O., Abran, A., Constantinides, C. (eds.) Software Engineering Research, Management and Applications 2010. Studies in Computational Intelligence, vol. 296, pp. 163–177. Springer, Heidelberg (2010). https://doi.org/10.1007/978-3-642-13273-5_11
26. Plosz, S., Varga, P.: Security and safety risk analysis of vision guided autonomous vehicles. In: 2018 IEEE Industrial Cyber-Physical Systems (ICPS), pp. 193–198 (2018). https://doi.org/10.1109/ICPHYS.2018.8387658
27. Sawilla, R., Defence R&D Canada Ottawa.: Googling attack graphs. Technical memorandum. Defence R&D Canada - Ottawa (2007)
28. Sheyner, O.M.: Scenario Graphs and Attack Graphs. PhD thesis, School of Computer Science, Pittsburgh, PA, USA, 2004. AAI3126929
29. Siveroni, I., Zisman, A., Spanoudakis, G.: A UML-based static verification framework for security. Requir. Eng. **15**, 95–118 (2010)
30. Solhaug, B., Seehusen, F.: Model-driven risk analysis of evolving critical infrastructures. J. Ambient Intell. Humanized Comput. **5**(2), 187–204 (2014). ISSN 1868–5137
31. Vijayakumar, H., Jakka, G., Rueda, S., Schiffman, J., Jaeger, T.: Integrity walls: finding attack surfaces from mandatory access control policies. In: Proceedings of the 7th ACM Symposium on Information, Computer and Communications Security (ASIACCS 12), pp. 75–76. ACM (2012)

Intruder Vehicle Detection During a Platoon Joining Maneuver

Haifa Gharbi[1]($\boxtimes$)(iD), Imen Jemili[2](iD), and Sabra Mabrouk[2](iD)

[1] Polytechnique of Montreal, Montreal, Canada
haifa.gharbi@polymtl.ca
[2] Faculty of Sciences of Bizerte, Bizerte, Tunisia
{imen.jemili,sabra.mabrouk}@fsb.ucar.tn

Abstract. To perform the different platoon maneuvers such as join-ing, merging, splitting, etc., platoon communication requires consider-able cooperation among platoon members. The joining operation is the most difficult to achieve when a new member wants to insert itself into the middle of the platoon. Indeed, some interferences due to the intrusion of an unwanted vehicle in the middle of the platoon lead to the aborting of the joining maneuver by the eligible vehicle and to communication prob-lems between the already existing members. In this context, we propose a Visual based method for Intruder vehicle Detection, denoted "VID". The main idea is to detect and classify vehicles (unwanted or not) dur-ing the join maneuver by analyzing the video recorded by the on-board cameras installed at the front of the platoon trucks. The performance of our method is tested and validated using videos of highway scenes in different weather conditions (sunny, rainy, cloudy). The obtained results show that VID can identify the intruder with rates higher than 89% and 95% for precision and recall respectively.

Keywords: Platooning · Join-maneuver · ROI extraction · Vehicle detection · Logo classification

1 Introduction

According to Bloomberg, the number of vehicles will climb by 35% by 2040 [1], as illustrated in Fig. 1. This increasing number of circulating vehicles worldwide leads to a considerable expansion of road traffic, which inevitably causes more and more traffic jams. In fact, as the growth rate of vehicles is faster than highway construction, it can lead to traffic congestion, energy waste, longer travel time, more accidents, and more pollution; these critical issues lead to health problems [2,3]. Nowadays, people aim to improve road capacity, traffic flow, and make travel safer and more comfortable [3–7]. An effective way to mitigate the mentioned problems is to shift from individual to cooperative driving, called also platoon-based driving.

Platooning is an Intelligent Transport System (ITS) application [8] which has emerged as a promising solution for traffic management in highways. Truck

© The Author(s), under exclusive license to Springer Nature Switzerland AG 2024
I. Jemili et al. (Eds.): DiCES-N 2023, CCIS 2041, pp. 83–115, 2024.
https://doi.org/10.1007/978-3-031-52823-1_5

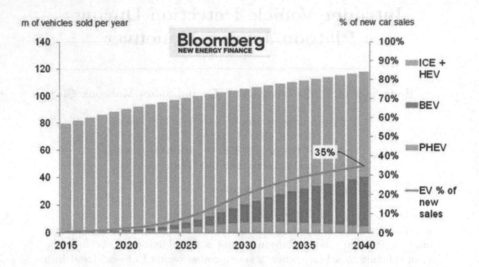

Fig. 1. The estimation of vehicles sales from 2015–2040 [1].

platoon is often defined as a convoy of vehicles which are traveling together in a tightly spaced group (platoon) with automated velocity and steering control. The vehicle platoon is commonly composed of a leader and one or more followers, called also platoon members. Figure 2 illustrates an example of a platoon of four heavy duty vehicles on a highway: one platoon leader (the first one) and three platoon followers. The leader vehicle performs as a chief and therefore the vehicles following it at the rear can act and suits changes in its movement, like lane changing, braking, etc. The leader also takes the responsibility of keeping the stability of the whole platooning by specifying the appropriate speed, distance between vehicles and therefore the relevant direction to follow; this information is communicated to all the members. It is also the responsible for coordinating the different maneuvers like join, leave, split, dissolve, etc.

Join maneuver occur when a truck tries to be a part of an already established platoon. The most important aspect of the Join maneuver is the insert position. In fact, different situations can occur such as back (tail) join, front join and middle join. The leave maneuver takes place when a given vehicle wants to exit the platoon (e.g. reaching its destination). The leader is informed first and the involved vehicle waits for the response before taking manual control and changing lanes. Then, the vehicles in front and behind this vehicle open a gap for safety reasons. When this vehicle leaves, they return to the imposed distance of the platoon. The merge maneuver allows the joining of two platoons, having the same destination, to form a single platoon. The process is usually initiated by the back platoon leader and then the front platoon leader decides to simply accept or reject the request. Split maneuver takes place when several vehicles want to exit the platoon in order to create a new one having another leader. The Dissolve maneuver occurs when the leader decides to separate the

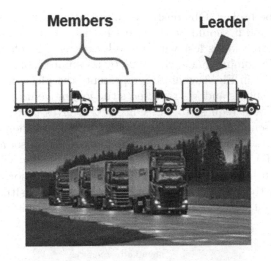

Fig. 2. Example of vehicle platooning.

entire platoon in several situations; for example, the platoon leader may quit
the platoon if there are obstacles on the road ahead or all vehicles have left the
platoon. The leader can only switch to manual driving mode after all followers
have acknowledged the order to leave the platoon. In our work, we particularly
focus on join maneuver. The traffic context should be taken into account in order
to execute this maneuver. In fact, it may require vehicles to accelerate, decel-
erate or change lanes; these different actions can disturb the driving conditions
of nearby vehicles. Besides, these neighboring vehicles may interfere with a platooning maneuver and delay its execution. Any vehicle, being in the trajectory
of the vehicles participating in the maneuver, represents an obstacle for a platooning operation which can be a risk for its safe execution. The interference
caused by such vehicles can delay the successful execution of the maneuver, and
can also impact the traffic flow and speed. Besides, another important aspect of
the join maneuver is the platoon ordering. The most simple and easy solution
of all is to make vehicles join the back (tail) of the platoon. However, joining
the platoon at the front is the hardest scenario since it requires roles change
in the platoon (a new Leader should be chosen). Moreover, allowing vehicles
to fit into any other position in the platoon permits members to be ordered
according to one of several parameters such as engine, weight or braking performance, aerodynamics, distance to be traveled, etc. However, the possibility that
an unauthorized vehicle enters the gap created by the members is high which can
lead to the aborting of the join maneuver. In fact, an unintended vehicle in the
middle of a platoon distorts the communication among the platoon members as
this intruder does not take part in platoon communication, and can cause a high
PLR (packet loss ratio). In this case, the maneuver cannot be performed by the
authorized vehicle and in the extreme cases (for example high traffic densities)

the platoon may be broken. Obviously, communication failures will also hamper the maneuvering, and it should be checked whether the maneuver can be safely aborted when information is lost without endangering the vehicles occupants.

An example of a joining maneuver made by an unintentional or unauthorized vehicle is illustrated in Fig. 3 where PL represents the platoon leader, v1 to v4 are the platoon members and M1 represents the joining vehicle. In the first step, M1 needs to send join request to PL. Once PL receives this request, it checks M1 location and sends a slow-down command to V3 in order to create a gap (small distance) and allow M1 to fit into the platoon. Even so, an unauthorized vehicle (red vehicle) can overtake it and enters into this gap which can distort the communication between V2 and V3 because this unauthorized vehicle does not participate in the communication of the platoon. This situation forces the PL to abort the join.

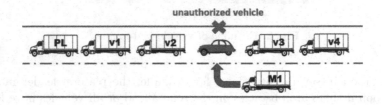

Fig. 3. Interference caused by an unauthorized vehicle entered.

In this context, authors in [9] surveyed the interference that can be generated by any unauthorized vehicle entering the platoon. Although, four scenarios are analyzed which are distant truck interference, close truck interference, car interference, and channel impairments, no solutions are proposed. The car interference is the most critical scenario, it can occur whenever a human-driven car occupies the gap vacated for the authorized vehicle. Authors in [10] presented an algorithm which is able to identify any interference caused by an unintended vehicle entered into the opened gap. The main goal of this algorithm is to first split the platoon at the intrusion point and then merge sub-platoons. In the second step, the radar distance with the GPS position, sent by the authorized vehicle, are compared to identify the vehicle entering the gap of platoon and verify the identity of the new member in order to ensure a successful termination of the operation. If it does not match, an intrusion is detected. Authors in [11] proposed a platoon management protocol for VANET and then the three basic platoon maneuvers are simulated namely joining, splitting, and lane changing. The authors also explained three platooning scenarios which are: the leave of the leader, the leave of a follower, and entry at the platoon tail. The developed protocol takes into account five different variables that any platoon enabled vehicle should have, namely vehicle ID, platoon ID, platoon depth, platoon size and platoon members. However, the presented protocol has some limitations namely the high delay during platoon merge maneuver. Moreover, the proposed approach for the platoon merge can only perform rear-end merge. Authors in [12] developed a hybrid controller for joining and splitting operations. The continuous-time system handles vertical control, and the discrete event supervisor decides the join and split operations. However, this method often loses connections in high vehicle dense areas which leads to high packet loss ratio (PLR). Authors in [13] proposed a cooperative platoon maneuver switching model for the discrete cooperative maneuver such as join and split based on hybrid automata to improve the utilization of road infrastructure resources. But this proposed protocol suffers from high latency and frequent loss of connections.

In this context, our goal is to address the joining operation, which is the most difficult to perform when a new member wants to insert himself in the middle of the platoon due to possible interference from other vehicles. We want to identify if there is an intrusion of an unwanted vehicle in the middle of the platoon. The main contributions of this work are:

- We conducted a systematic literature review including the most appropriate approaches for vehicle detection and classification.
- We proposed a Visual based method for Intruder vehicle Detection, denoted "VID". It consists of three main steps: (i) Road area extraction based on color features, (ii) Vehicle detection based on Haar-like features and AdaBoost classifier, and (iii) Identification of authorized vehicles based on the logo situated on the rear area of each truck using CNN.
- We evaluated the performance of the proposed framework using video sequences taken with front-view cameras in different cities; the scenes involve highway trips in various weather conditions (sunny, rainy, snowy and cloudy).

The rest of this paper is organized as follows: in Sect. 2, a description of the related state of the art is given. In Sect. 3, our proposed framework is detailed. In Sect. 4, the obtained results are presented. Finally, we conclude our work.

2 Related Work

2.1 Vehicle Detection

For many years, vehicle detection has been an important part of the intelligent vehicle system. Each operation of vehicle detection needs an effective collection of environmental data which depends on the high-precision and high-reliability of sensors. The deployed sensors in this context can be divided into two kinds: active sensors such as Lidar, radar, ultrasonic, etc. and passive sensors such stereo cameras, monocular camera, omnidirectional cameras, event cameras, infrared cameras etc. [14].

Indeed cameras are the most commonly used passive sensors in the field of vehicle detection thanks to their ability to generate a high resolution images containing environmental information like texture, color, and so on. Moreover, they have good coverage, small size and low cost. Various vehicle detection techniques using images recorded by cameras have been proposed in the literature.

Usually, the visual based methods can be done in one-stage or two stages. One stage methods do not require candidate regions extraction that should be analyzed for vehicle detection. Omitting region extraction allows faster processing, which is ideal for time-sensitive applications; however, the detection accuracy is low and the robustness is poor. Two-stage methods requires a Hypothesis Generation (HG) step and Hypothesis Verification (HV) step. A set of candidate regions (called region of interests: ROIs), that may contain vehicles in the captured image, are generated in the HG step. Then, the vehicle can be easily identified in this ROIs in the HV step.

Hypothetical Generation Methods (HG). The main purpose of the HG step is to quickly locate the vehicle position in an image for further exploration. The hypothetical positions discovered in the HG step are fed into the HV step, which performs a test to check the exactness of these hypotheses. In the literature, various HG approaches have been proposed and they can be classified into the following three categories: Knowledge-based, motion-based and stereo-based methods. The first category uses prior knowledge of some vehicle features to estimate the car's position in the image. The most commonly used features include: symmetry, shadows under the vehicles, color, geometrical features (such as corners, horizontal and vertical edges), texture, and vehicle lights. [43] proposed a new method for detecting vehicles that are fully/partially visible from the rear view. The method is divided into two main steps. First, the two parts of the rear view of a vehicle are detected using Haar-like features and Adaboost cascade classifiers. Second, the symmetry is used to detect vehicles that are fully visible. Similarly, [44] proposed an algorithm that uses two stages to detect vehicles. A new vehicle enhancement filter based on the vehicle's structural information is used to identify potential vehicle locations. Then, the identified locations are refined using bilateral symmetry of the vehicles with respect to an axis. [45] proposed a vehicle detection method for urban traffic using shadow under vehicles. The main idea of this method is to compare pixel properties across the vertical intensity gradients caused by shadows on the road and then perform intensity thresholding and shape recognition. [46] explored the use of color information as a hint for detecting vehicles. They proposed a model to find vehicles' colors in order to quickly detect possible vehicle candidates. But, using color in vehicles detection is uncommon due to its variability under different weather and light conditions. [47] proposed a method to detect vehicles from the headlights and taillights using image segmentation and pattern analysis. First, an automatic multi-level histogram threshold is applied to extract all bright objects. Second, these extracted bright objects are processed through spatial clustering in order to identify and classify moving vehicles. The method was finally tested and evaluated on real highways and urban roads and in different night's scenes. The knowledge-based approaches have the drawback of being sensitive to local/global picture changes such as pose, lighting, and partial occlusion.

Motion-based methods do not need any prior knowledge; these methods extract vehicles that are distinguished from the fixed background by their motion. Generally, a static camera is used to model the background and segment the moving foreground objects. Such an approach does not require pretraining and can recognize previously unseen moving objects. State of the art methods include frame differencing, background subtraction and optical flow methods. [48] proposed a vehicle detection approach using the traditional two-frame difference method. This method can easily separate the background of current frame occluded by previous frame, and obtains a good result with a low computational cost. The main problem is that when the detected object has a uniform gray-scale, the overlapping part of the moving objects in the image will appear "blank". To solve this problem, the three-frame difference method was established by [49] and then improved by [50] to better solve the problem of "blank holes" in the image. [52] also proposed a new system that can detect moving objects in complex road scenes by implementing an advanced background subtraction method. [53] used information provided by Radar and camera to implement an optical flow method to detect vehicles. The radar sensor can detect the same vehicle multiple times, while the optical flow method can only detect vehicles with a significant speed difference compared with the ego-vehicle. [51] proposed an effective vehicle counting where Kalman filter algorithm is used to count and track the multiple moving vehicles in complex traffic scenes. Proposed methods in this context rely on various forms of background subtraction, making them unsuitable for cameras with significant ego-motion on the vehicle (the motion of monocular moving camera with arbitrary translation and rotation). However, proposed methods in this context rely on various forms of background subtraction, making them unsuitable for cameras with significant ego-motion on the vehicle (the motion of monocular moving camera with arbitrary translation and rotation).

Stereo-based methods represent another kind of HG method, in which information's collected by stereo vision is used to detect vehicles. In the literature, two different methods have been established. The first one uses the disparity map, while the second one uses the anti-perspective transformation. In order to detect vehicles, several methods based on disparity maps have been proposed. [54] introduced a new method to detect and track vehicles using a semi-dense disparity map. The mean-shift algorithm is also used in order to cluster and track these vehicles. [55] used the disparity maps technique to design a method for detecting vehicles and estimating their motion states, in which a simple iterative clustering is combined with optical flow. [56] trained a CNN in order to generate the semantic maps, then clustering based on the Depth-first search (DFS) algorithm is used for vehicle detection. [57] used images collected by a camera installed behind a car's rear view mirror for distance detection. After converting the images to an aerial view, and restoring information about the road surface, the converted IPM image will be used to estimate the distance of the target vehicle. The biggest problem is that the conversion into Inverse Perspective Mapping (IPM) image means that the size has changed, so the system cannot detect certain target vehicles in the IPM image. [58] combined IPM with CNN for estimating the position, size, and direction of vehicles.

Hypothesis Verification Methods (HV). Hypothesis verification (HV) methods include tests allowing verifying the correctness of vehicle location hypothesis, previously generated in the HG step. Therefore, the output of the HV methods is an accurate "car" or "non-car" automatic classification. Over time, several HV methods have been presented, which can be divided into two main categories [17]: template-based methods and appearance-based methods. The template-based methods use the vehicle class's predefined patterns to perform correlation between the selected image locations and the predefined templates. The appearance-based methods learn the vehicle class attributes from a series of training images that should reflect the appearance's allowable variability. In general, the variability of the non-vehicle class should be modelled to improve the performance. An illustration of a set of training images is presented in Fig. 4. Initially, a large set of training images should be obtained, where each training image is defined by a collection of features. Then, either by training a classifier or by modeling the probability distribution of the features in each class, the decision boundary between non-vehicle and vehicle classes is learned.

Fig. 4. Examples of car and non-car images used for training.

For template-based methods, some of the templates proposed in the literature represent the vehicle class "loosely," while others are more detailed. [59] proposed a HV algorithm based on the presence of license plates and rear windows. This can be considered as a loose template of the vehicle class. [60] proposed a template based on the observation that the rear view of a vehicle has a "U" shape which describes the one horizontal edge, two vertical edges, and two corners connecting the horizontal and vertical edges. The image region was considered as a vehicle, if the'U' shape is detected. The same system is proposed by [62] using a template, based on the fact that the visual appearance of an object depends on its distance from the camera. Consequently, a two slightly different generic object (vehicle) models are used, one for nearby objects and another for distant objects. However, this proposed method raises the question of what model to use in a specific location. [61] proposed a new system to recognize vehicles using a very loose template. Another system is proposed by [63] where distance-dependent sub-sampling was performed before the verification step, instead of working with different generic models. [64] proposed a system for night-time detection of vehicles using morphological operators. A template, called "moving edge closure," was also used and fitted to groups of moving points. An edge detection is performed on the area covered by the detected moving points, followed by the external edge connection in order to get the moving edge closure. The vehicle is detected if the size of the moving edge closure was within a predefined range. Moreover, a rather loose template is used by [65] in which hypotheses were generated on the basis of road position and perspective constraints. The template contained a priori knowledge about vehicles: A vehicle is usually symmetric, characterized by a rectangular bounding box which satisfies specific aspect ratio constraints. In the first step, the hypothesized region was checked for the presence of two corners representing the bottom of the bounding box. However, because of the nature of the template matching methods, most papers proposed over the years do not report quantitative results.

For appearance-based methods, several feature extraction methods have been proposed Over the years in the context of vehicle detection. Based on the method used, the features extracted can be classified as either local or global. Global features are obtained by considering all the pixels in an image. [66] proposed a solution to recognize vehicles using nearest-neighbor classifier. However, the used training database was too small, which makes it difficult to draw any useful conclusions. Another solution proposed by [67] for object detection based on global features. The approach builds a distribution-based model of objects patterns, and learns from examples a set of distance parameters to distinguish between "object" and "non object" window patterns. An inherent problem with global feature extraction approaches is that they are sensitive to local or global image variations (e.g., pose changes, illumination changes, and partial occlusion). On the other hand, local features are less sensitive to these effects. Moreover, geometric information and constraints in the configuration of different local features can be utilized either explicitly or implicitly. [68] proposed a general method for object detection applied to front and rear views of vehicles. A complete set of Haar wavelet coefficients of certain scales are computed and a SVM (Support Vector Machine) is trained to classify vehicles (car and non-car). This representation provided a richer model and spatial resolution and it was suitable for capturing complex patterns. [69] proposed a method for rear-view vehicle detection using wavelet parameters as input vector, and performed a SVM-based classifier to verify the candidate solutions. They went further to assert that the actual values of the wavelet coefficients are not very important for vehicle detection. Furthermore, [69] consider the problem of rear-view vehicle detection from gray-scale images. They combined Haar wavelet with Gabor features to describe the properties of a vehicle and SVM for classification. [70] used a vision-based vehicle detection system. The symmetry of the HOG features extracted in a given image patch, along with the HOG features themselves, was used for vehicle detection. [71] proposed a vision-based vehicle detection system particularly in the blind-spot area for driving assistance through hazard warning. In this method, a camera captures the images of the blind-spot area and the video stream is then analyzed to warn the driver if a vehicle is detected; the driver will consequently give up the lane changing decision to avoid an accident. The main drawback of the local features is that they are quite slow to compute. In recent years, there has been a transition from complex image features such as Gabor filters and HOG to simpler and efficient feature sets for vehicle detection. Haar-like features are sensitive to vertical, horizontal, and symmetric structures, and they can be computed efficiently, making them well suited for real-time detection of vehicles [18].

Features for Vehicle Detection. Features can be represented as functions of the original measurement variables which could be used for pattern recognition and/or classification. Feature extraction refers to the process of transforming training samples in something like a feature vector that can fulfills the classifier's input requirements [19]. Overall, the main goal of features extraction would be to make object identification and classification more effective and efficient. To produce superior classification results, the design and selection of features are especially critical. To maximize training efficiency, a fine feature should comprise the majority of the vehicle's design and be the simple as possible. The extracted features can usually be used for object detection or target tracking, such as human faces, vehicles, pedestrians, traffic signs, etc. Commonly used feature extraction methods in the literature include: Haar-like features and HOG (Histogram of Oriented Gradients) and LBP (Local Binary Pattern).

- **Haar-like features:**
  Haar-like features (also called Haar features) were first proposed by Viola and Jones [20] to detect human faces. They can provide information about the gray-scale distribution of two adjacent areas in the image. For a variety of reasons, it is widely assumed that detection algorithms based on Haar-like features are more efficient and effective than other approaches that process pixels directly [21].
  [22] introduced two kinds of original Haar features which are shown in Fig. 5(a) and (b). The two rectangles which are left-right of the feature shown in Fig. 5(a) can have also the "up-down" position. [20] extended Haar-like feature with three rectangles, displayed in Fig. 5 (c). The three types of rotational features enriched by [23] are shown in Fig. 5(d), (e) and (f).
  Each Haar-like feature contains at least two connected "black" and "white" rectangles. In order to calculate the value of each Haar-like feature, (Eq. 1) is used where f(x) represents the difference between both the gray values of the pixels in the black and white rectangles when added together.

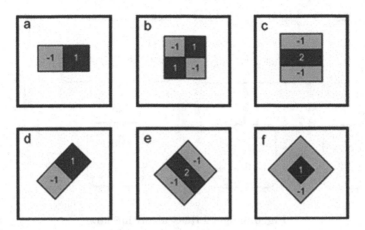

Fig. 5. Example of Haar-like features: (a) and (b) illustrate Haar-like features provided by [22]. [20] developed a Haar-like featue with three rectangles in (c). The rotational features of [23] are seen in (d–f).

$$f(x) = \sum_{black rectangle} (pixel value) - \sum_{white rectangle} (pixel value). \quad (1)$$

If three rectangles appear in one Haar feature which shown in Fig. 5(c) or (e), default integer weights need to be assigned for each rectangle to ensure an equal number of pixels in black and white regions [24]. The default weights assigned in Fig. 5(c) and (e) are −1, 2 and −1.

- **Histogram of Oriented Gradients (HOG):**
In recent years, object detectors based on edge analysis have been used in many detection tasks, and these detectors provide valuable information about objects of interest. In this field, the Histogram of Oriented Gradients (HOG) is considered as one of the popular feature descriptors used in image processing and computer vision for the purpose of target detection. This method is introduced first by Dalal and Triggs [25] who tackled the problem of pedestrian detection.

The HOG descriptor's main benefit is that it could accurately represent the contour and edge features of elements other than humans, such as vehicles, animals, and so on. The HOG features extraction and target detection process is depicted in Fig. 6 using sevetal classification algorithm such as SVM and AdaBoost.

Initially, the normalized input image is scanned based on the sliding window, which is divided later into many blocks (called cells). Then, a histogram of gradient orientations is accumulated to each cell. The obtained histogram is normalized by accumulating the energy of the local histogram on the block; the result is used to normalize all the cells in the block in order to have a better illumination invariance. Next, the HOG features (histograms already normalized) are collected on the detection window. The collected features are

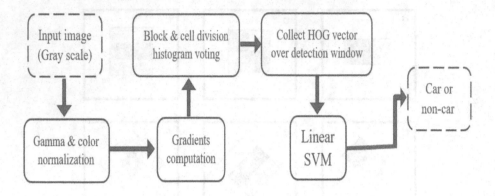

Fig. 6. Original HOG algorithm flow.

fed to a classification algorithm (linear SVM) for object/non-object classification.

– **Local Binary Patterns (LBP):**

[26] introduced Local Binary Patterns (LBP) as another powerful and effective local descriptor for micro-structures of images in computer vision. It can be represented as an efficient image feature which can transform an image into an array or image of integer labels describing the small scale appearances. These labels are therefore added to the image for further processing. Face recognition, texture analysis, object detection and tracking and several applications proposed over the years employ LBP.

A few years later, some improvements were made to LBP. A generic LBP operator is proposed by [27]; its particularity that it uses quarters of different sizes (not only 3×3 pixel block) to capture the main features at different scales. In addition, this improved solution has been extended from a rectangular to a circular domain allowing to select any number of neighborhoods at any distance. Another improved LBP solution proposed by [28] is called Multi-Block Local Binary Pattern Feature (MB-LBP). The particularity of MB-LBP is that it is defined by comparing the value of the central block with the values of its eight neighboring blocks.

2.2 Vehicle Classification

The main goal of a classifier is to use the extracted features in order to identify whether or not the input sub-window includes an object. Given a set of training examples, every one can be identified as belonging to one of the K categories. The algorithm of classification can construct a new model that can assign new examples that are not training examples to one category or other categories. In the literature, several classification algorithms have been proposed. The most two popular algorithms are AdaBoost and Support Vector Machine (SVM).

Adaptive Boosting (AdaBoost). The AdaBoost classifier can be presented as a machine learning algorithm, which was first proposed by Yoav Freund and Schapire [29]. It was creatively applied to detect human faces by [20], thus opening a new chapter in image processing technology. The feature sets like Haar, LBP and HOG are extremely enormous. For example, for HOG, there are nearly 576 features, while LBP can reach 3600 depending on the version. For the Haar features, when the window size is 20×20, there are 45891 features, and if all possible parameters (position, scale, and type) are considered, more than 160,000 features can be reached. It is clear that all these descriptors contain a big number of useless and redundant information. In this context, AdaBoost is a powerful classifier that can be used to avoid these redundant features and pick only effective and useful features and solve the following three basic tasks:

- Evaluate and select only the significant and effective input features.
- Construct the (simple or weak) classifiers, where each classifier is constructed based on only a single candidate feature.
- Use the boosting process to make the selected weak classifier stronger

The weak learning algorithm aims to select a single image feature that produces a good result. AdaBoost can be defined as a combination of a weak classifiers in a weighted voting machine, and it can perform well in various fields. Figure 7 shows clearly architecture of AdaBoost classifier.

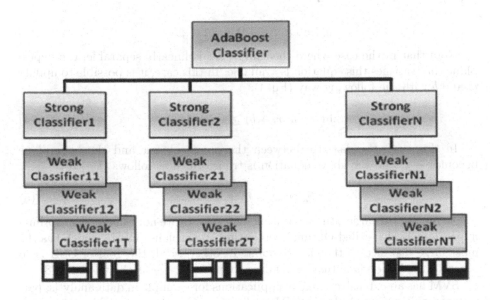

Fig. 7. The architecture of the AdaBoost classifier.

The weak learning algorithm is intended in order to choose one image feature that can yield the most effective result. For each feature and in order to minimize the number of mis-classified examples, an optimal threshold should be generated [20] and defined by (Eq. 2).

$$h_j(x) = \begin{cases} 1 \& if p_j f_i(x) < p_{j\Theta_j} \\ 0 \; otherwise \end{cases} \tag{2}$$

Where, each weak classifier $h_j(x)$ is composed of features f_i, a threshold Θ_j and a coefficient factor p_j indicating the direction of the inequality, and x represents the input image sub-window.

Support Vector Machine (SVM). Support Vector Machines (SVM) represent another popular and powerful pattern recognition classification algorithm proposed by [30]. The main goal of SVM is to find the optimal solution for class splitting and it has the separating hyperplane as result. To obtain the optimal results, SVM has some parameters to be adjusted. Suppose we have the following example of a training database with a size of N: (x_i, y_i), $i \in [1, N]$ and x_i represents a descriptor vector, belonging to the class marked by $y_i \in [-1, 1]$. This class is to represent the binary result (-1 means false/negative, 1 means true/positive). The main goal of classification is to construct a hyperplane equation that divides the database set: the first side includes all the points labeled with $y_i = 1$ and the other side contains the points labeled by $y_i = -1$. More precisely, two parameters w and b should be found to satisfy the following inequality (Eq. 3):

$$y_i(w.x_i) + b > 0, i = 1, ..., N \tag{3}$$

Note that in the case where the sample set is linearly separable, the hyperplane that satisfies this equation is available. In this case, it is possible to update w and b with the following way (Eq. 4):

$$\min_{1 \le i \le N} y_i(w.x_i + b) \ge 1, i = 1, ..., N \tag{4}$$

In this case, the distance between the points closest and the hyperplane becomes $\frac{1}{\|w\|}$, and the above equation is transformed as follows (Eq. 5):

$$y_i(w.x_i + b) \ge 1 \quad \forall i \tag{5}$$

As mentioned earlier, the separating hyperplanes are not unique. The optimal hyperplane is also called Optimal Separating Hyperplane (OSH), which has the most large distance to the closest point. In other word, the goal of OSH is to separate the hyperplane that maximizes the margin $\frac{2}{\|w\|}$ as shown in Fig. 8.

SVM has an extensive range of applications for example in data analysis, pattern recognition, etc. A classic SVM application example proposed by the author in [25] used a locally normalized Histogram of Oriented Gradient (HOG) descriptors are used and SVM is employed as a classifier in order to achieve an excellent pedestrian detector. Over the years, some application based on SVM have been

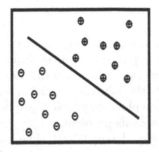 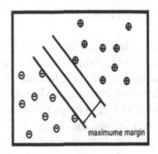

Fig. 8. An example of optimal separating hyperplane in 2D.

improved, such as in traffic sign classification [31], vehicle detection [32], pedestrian detection [33] and many other fields, which means that SVM has excellent capabilities in image recognition and classification.

Other Classifiers. In addition to SVM and AdaBoost, other classifiers are used. Some of the most used classifiers are K-Nearest Neighbor (KNN) and Convolutional Neural Network (CNN).

- **K-Nearest Neighbor (KNN)**
  KNN can be represented as a non-parametric algorithm that is dubbed the "lazy algorithm" due its low complexity in comparison to other classification algorithms. The data is classified using the KNN algorithm's closest neighbor features. The locate the nearest point between the features, the algorithm uses the Euclidean distance method.
- **Convolutional Neural Network (CNN)**
  Authors in [34] introduced Convolutional Neural Networks as a method for visual pattern recognition. However, due to the development of high-performance of Graphics Processing Unit (GPU) architectures, they have only recently gained traction in the scientific community [35]. A CNN takes an input image, that has typically had some minimal preprocessing and runs it through a series of transformation layers to create an image class prediction. In the past ten years, neural networks (NN) have become popular, which can achieve nonlinear decision boundaries [17]. But the neural network needs to perform parameter adjustment calculations, so it is very time-consuming. Thanks to advances in deep learning technology, Convolutional Neural Networks (CNN) have achieved considerable success in visual vehicle detection solutions. [58] used the R-CNN deep learning method to train their model and apply it to the vehicle detection process. For vehicle classification, [37] employs Fast R-CNN, which is divided into two parts: region proposal and object recognition. But this method is slow and has limited accuracy because it is very time-consuming to generate object recommendations and it is not optimized during the training process.

3   VID Framework

During a platoon joining operation, three possible scenarios can be distinguished: joining the platoon from the tail, joining the platoon from the front and entering into the middle of the platoon. In this work, we focus on this latter scenario which is the most complicated one. In fact, the join maneuver is aborted when an unintended vehicle enters the midst of the platoon, which disrupts communication among platoon members. To overcome this problem, we propose a Visual based method for Intruder vehicle Detection, denoted VID. The main idea is to exploit the video sequences provided by front-view cameras to delineate the region where authorized vehicles are expected to fit during the join maneuver and to check these newly joined vehicles. As illustrated in Fig. 9, our approach comprises three phases: ROI identification, vehicle detection and classification. To get rid of irrelevant objects, we first proceed with a road extraction process. Then, we perform a ROI delineation to detect and check all vehicles entering the platoon gap. If a truck is detected, recognition of the logo on its back allows confirming whether it is an authorized truck or not.

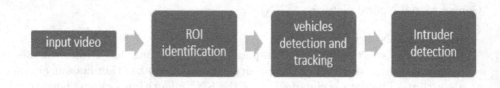

Fig. 9. Overview of VID approach.

In the following detail of our proposed framework by identifying its main components and used methods.

3.1   Region of Interest Extraction

The basic idea is to allow platoon trucks to keep an eye on the front region where any new vehicle could be inserted. By analyzing video stream provided by a front-view camera, we aim to identify the ROI referring to the road area in front of the truck. To this end, we first perform a road extraction step by exploiting the color features related to the road, usually in shades of gray. Then, we detect lines as the ROI is delineated with lane markers, commonly in white or yellow [38]. As shown in Fig. 10, this approach includes three main steps: road extraction, lane detection and ROI identification.

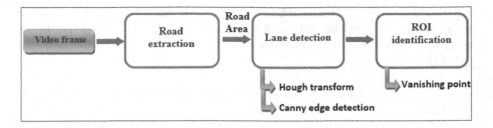

Fig. 10. Overview of the ROI extraction method.

3.2 Vehicle Detection

Once the road area is extracted and the ROI is identified, it now becomes easy to detect any vehicle entering the platoon gap during the join maneuver and classify it as a car or truck. For this purpose, we use Haar-like features and the Adaboost cascade classifier, described below.

– Features extraction

Our method uses the five main Haar features shown in Fig. 11 in order to determine the feature values of all samples. The complete set of rectangular features for a vehicle sample of size 24 × 24 is rather big (up to 162,336). As a result, the integral image is applied to compute these features quickly.

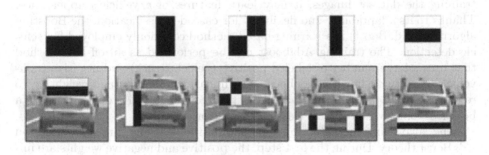

Fig. 11. Haar-like features suitable for vehicle rear view.

The integral value of each pixel in an integral image is computed as below (Eq. 6):

$$ii\left(x,y\right) = \sum_{x'\leq x, y'\leq y} i\left(x',y'\right) \qquad (6)$$

where $ii\left(x',y'\right)$ represents the integral value of pixel (x,y) and $i\left(x',y'\right)$ represents the gray value of pixel (x',y') in the original image. The Haar feature may be extracted quickly using the integral image. The intensity of the shadow region can be depicted in [39] as illustrated in Fig. 12. Only six points in the integral image are required to compute the difference between two neighboring rectangles.

$$ii\left(x_A,y_A\right) + ii\left(x_D,y_D\right) - ii\left(x_B,y_B\right) - ii\left(x_C,y_C\right) \tag{7}$$

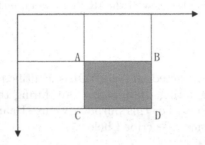

Fig. 12. Intensity calculation of shadow region.

– **Vehicle classification**

In order to detect vehicles, we use Adaboost as classifier in our method. From training the dataset images, it may learn features of a vehicle's appearance. Thanks to its adaptability and flexibility for cascade classification, the Boosting algorithm (AdaBoost) is a learning-based method commonly employed for vehicle detection. The training Adaboost can be performed as an off-line method that uses a large number of labeled positive (vehicle/truck) and negative (non-vehicle/non-truck) images. Adaboost uses linear combination and weighting to remove weak filters from the Haar-like extracted features in order to produce a better classifier with a lowest classification error.

The algorithm presented by [40] shows the learning process based on AdaBoost theory. During the first step, the positive and negative weights are initialized. Then, the weights will be updated (using an iterative loop). The learning process usually excludes a large set of available features, but only focuses on a few numbers of significant features to ensure a rapid classification. According to this algorithm, for every step in the boosting process, only the new effective weak classifier is selected. Then, all the best weak classifiers are selected and combined into a strong classifier.

– **Intruder detection**

In order to classify the detected truck (authorized or not), we use a logo detection and recognition method that can locate and recognize the logo on the rear view of the truck. To this end, we have recall to convolutional neural networks (CNN). CNN allows an image to be examined pixel by pixel and to generate models that learn patterns in the pixel arrangements. Each image in the dataset has a correct classification that the model will use to train itself by comparing to the prediction. For any correct prediction, the error will be 0, otherwise it is 1.

In our method, CNN is used to learn the content of images. Each image will be sent through a convolutional layer first. Sections of pixels will all be filtered and sent through the pooling layer, then analyzed and compared to a desired result to make a prediction of whether the image falls into a certain category. The CNN process is shown in Fig. 13.

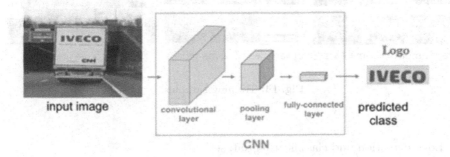

Fig. 13. The CNN process.

4   Performance Evaluation

Our objective is to evaluate the performance of our method under different scenarios. The vehicle detection and classification algorithms were implemented in Python and the library OpenCV that supports image processing has been used. In the following, we present the different datasets and metrics used in this work, and then we expose the experimental results.

4.1   Datasets

We use three datasets:

– Lane detection dataset

We collected 80 online video sequences taken using front view cameras in highway sceneries in different cities (California, Turkey, Texas, Toronto, Seoul-Korea, Marysville-usa). These video sequences are divided into four categories depending on weather conditions (sunny, rainy, snowy and cloudy), and they include straight roads with solid and dash lines [38].

– Vehicle detection dataset

In order to verify the efficiency of the vehicle detection method, a total of 700 images are used; the dataset is composed of car and non-car and truck and non-truck. We consider 300 car samples, 200 truck samples and 200 negative samples. All images are normalized to a size of 30*30 pixels, and some of these data samples are shown in Fig. 14.

(a) Sample of some cars   (b) Samples of some trucks   (c) Negative images

Fig. 14. Training samples.

– Logo detection and classification dataset

In our experiment, the logo situated in the rear-view of each truck should be captured using the onboard-camera. The whole database contains 200 images which cover 2 logo categories (authorized and non-authorized), as shown in Fig. 15.

In logo detection step, logos were cropped from different back's truck images; data is prepared to build reliable and accurate logo detection system. These logo samples have been manually labeled and obtained from the internet. We divided the dataset into training and validation datasets, consisting of 120 images and 80 images respectively having 56 × 40 pixels.

a) Authorized logo samples   (b) Non-authorized logo samples

Fig. 15. Training Logo Samples.

4.2   Evaluation Metrics

In this evaluation step, we illustrated our results using the following metrics.

- **Recall rate:** Measures the proportion of cases that have been correctly detected. It is calculated as follows:

$$Recall = \frac{TP}{TP + TN} \tag{8}$$

- **Precision rate:** measures the proportion of positive cases actually detected. It is expressed by:

$$Precision = \frac{TP}{TP + FP} \tag{9}$$

- **F-measure:** It is the average of precision and recall, it is computed as follows:

$$F - measure = 2 \times \frac{Recall \times Precision}{Recall + Precision} \tag{10}$$

Where:

- **True Positive (TP):** represents the proportion of positive cases that were correctly identified, (Correctly predicting a label).
- **False Positive (FP):** represents the proportion of negatives cases that were incorrectly classified as positive, (Falsely predicting a label).
- **False Negative (FN):** represents the proportion of positives cases that were incorrectly classified as negative, (Missing label).
- **True Negative (TN):** represents the proportion of negatives cases that were classified correctly, (Correctly predicting the other label).

For lane detection experiments, since no negative data (i.e., ground-truth non-lane point) can be delimitated, (TN) rates are 0%.

4.3   Results

The different tests and results used to evaluate the effectiveness of our method are presented in this subsection.

- Region of interest extraction

Table 1 clearly illustrates the calculated recall, precision and accuracy rates for the various considered weathers conditions. On a sunny day, and as expected, the proposed method provides great results with rates over 90% for the three studied metrics. This is due to the fact that lane marks are easily recognizable. On cloudy days, the results are less satisfying. Similarly, on rainy days, performances decrease, with F-measure, recall and precision rates slightly around 60%. This is due to the interference of raindrops on the front windshield. In snowy conditions, our method gives lower percentages, with just 20% for F-measure,

Table 1. The proposed method performance according to weather conditions.

	Sunny %	Rainy %	Cloudy %	Snowy %
Recall	93	63	71	23
Precision	99	64	88	18
F - measure	96	63	78	20

23% for recall and 18% for precision. This might be explained by the fact that under such circumstances, the road is completely or partially covered with white snow, which distorts the road extraction and lane marks detection and leads to an increased false-positive number.

Some ROI detection results (green triangle) under different weather are presented in Fig. 16. The detection results appear to be excellent on sunny days (Fig. 16(a) and (b)), but less satisfying on sever conditions (Fig. 16(c), (d) and (e)). Our method fails to recognize all the lines, resulting in a visually misplaced ROI, as shown in (Fig. 16(f)).

– Vehicle detection

In this section, we compare our method against two other methods using the same classifier Adaboost but with different features namely LPB and HOG.

Table 2 presents the results while considering the whole image. Table 3 and the graphic in Fig. 17 represent the results while considering the extracted ROI. It is clear that results give excellent rates in sunny days in the two cases, especially when the Haar-like and AdaBoost algorithm are used with rates above 90%. For the cloudy and rainy days, the results are less satisfying. When the extracted ROI is taken into the account, the results become better for the three considered metrics. This is due to the decrease of the noise and the removal of the unwanted region as only the road area is processed in the image.

Figure 18 shows the different Confusion matrix of the three features using AdaBoost algorithm. The true positive rate (correctly detected vehicles) is high when Haar-like features are considered (Fig. 18(a)). When HOG is used (Fig. 18(b)), the falsely predicted vehicles is high. The LBP algorithm shows the worst result (Fig. 18(c)) with a high number of falsely detected or missing vehicles.

Results in Table 2 show that the algorithm combining Haar-like features and AdaBoost gives the best results even when we consider detection on the whole image with rates exceeding 76% for sunny days. Its performance decreases as expected in severe conditions but remains above the two other algorithms. The ROI extraction step improves results of all three algorithms. The Haar-like and AdaBoost method outperforms the other two algorithms in term of recall, precision with a success rate of over 90% for sunny days and even over 80% in cloudy days. These results could be explained by the fact that the Haar-like features are relatively resistant to noise and lighting changes because they calculate the gray level difference between the white and black rectangles. Moreover, Haar-like

Fig. 16. Result of ROI detection in different weather conditions.

Table 2. Testing results of different algorithms while considering the whole image.

	Number of videos	Method	Recall (%)	Precision(%)	F-measure(%)
Sunny	30	LBP + AdaBoost	63	67	68
		HOG + AdaBoost	70	75.2	73
		Haar + AdaBoost	79.7	81	76.3
Cloudy	20	LBP + AdaBoost	53	58	54
		HOG + AdaBoost	57	66.8	65
		Haar + AdatBoost	65.5	79.8	74.7
Rainy	10	LBP + AdaBoost	31.8	33.2	30
		HOG + AdaBoost	36	34.3	32.3
		Haar + AdaBoost	43	37	40

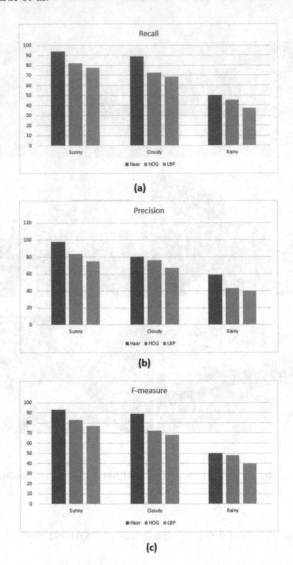

Fig. 17. Testing results of different algorithms: (a) LBP, (b) HOG, (c) Haar

Features are good at detecting edges and lines. The proposed method gives also the highest F1-measure; this metric is considered as a comprehensive evaluation index demonstrating the overall performance.

Figure 19 shows the detection results of our proposed car/truck detection method using Haar-like and AdaBoost classifier in different weathers condition.

– Logo classification

In order to check if the truck entering into the platoon gap is authorized or not, the logo situated in the back of this truck should be detected. In the

Table 3. Testing results of different algorithms while considering the extracted ROI.

	Number of videos	Method	Recall (%)	Precision(%)	F-measure(%)
Sunny	30	LBP + AdaBoost	72.3	75.7	77.5
		HOG + AdaBoost	80.7	83.5	83
		Haar + AdaBoost	90.2	98	93.1
Cloudy	20	LBP + AdaBoost	70.7	67.8	68.6
		HOG + AdaBoost	77.7	76.8	72.5
		Haar + AdatBoost	85.6	80.5	89.3
Rainy	10	LBP + AdaBoost	41.7	43.3	37
		HOG + AdaBoost	49.1	43.5	48
		Haar + AdaBoost	54.1	59.5	50.2

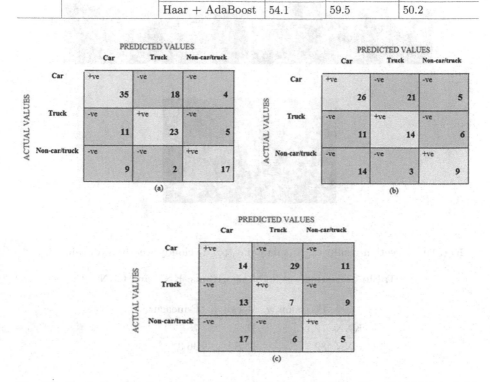

Fig. 18. Confusion Matrix using AdaBoost algorithm: (a) Haar-like; (b) HOG and (c) LBP.

experiment, two classification techniques were used namely the KNN and CNN, and the outcomes of these techniques were compared. Both techniques use the same training and testing data and operate in the same system environment. The K value in the KNN algorithm is fixed to 3. For CNN, 5 layers are used and each image is smoothed by a Gaussian filter with a 3*3 kernel and sigma value of 1. The different testing results of these methods are shown in Table 4 and in the graphic in Fig. 20. For CNN algorithm the results seem to be excellent with

Fig. 19. Detection result: (a, b) sunny day, (c, d) cloudy weather, (e) rainy day.

Table 4. Testing results of algorithms: KNN and CNN

	Precision %	Recall %	F-measure %
KNN	79.1	75.7	75
CNN	89.7	95.8	96.3

rates over 90% for the three studied metrics. For the KNN algorithm the results are less satisfying with rates around 70%.

Figure 21 shows the Confusion matrix for the used algorithm CNN and KNN. The correctly detected logo is high and the falsely detected and missing logos is low when CNN algorithm is used compared with the KNN algorithm.

The KNN classifier shows the worst performance with a precision, recall and F-measure of 79%, 75% and 75% respectively. However, the CNN rates were respectively 89%, 95% and 96%. The main advantage of CNN compared to KNN is that its computational efficiency. It conducts parameters sharing and employs convolution and pooling techniques to enables CNN models to operate on any

Testing results of KNN and CNN
120
100
80
60
40
20
0
Precision
Recall
F-measure
CNN
KNN

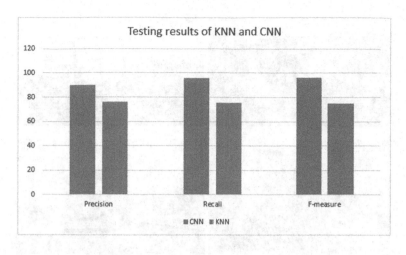

Fig. 20. Testing results of KNN and CNN.

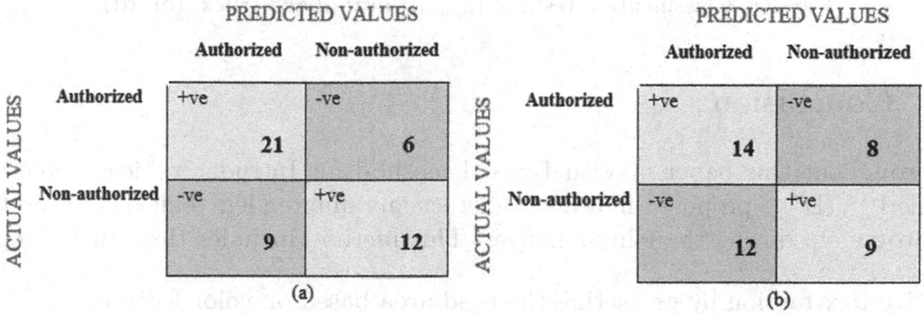

PREDICTED VALUES
Authorized
Non-authorized
ACTUAL VALUES
Authorized
Non-authorized
+ve
21
-ve
6
-ve
9
+ve
12
(a)
PREDICTED VALUES
Authorized
Non-authorized
ACTUAL VALUES
Authorized
Non-authorized
+ve
14
-ve
8
-ve
12
+ve
9
(b)

Fig. 21. Confusion Matrix for: (a) CNN; (b) KNN.

device, making them globally attractive. Moreover, it is highly powerful and efficient model that operates automated feature extraction with superhuman accuracy. CNN is better at classification and categorization and has excellent generalization abilities.

In our method, we use CNN to detect and classify the different logos situated in the rear view of each truck; some testing results of CNN are shown in Fig. 22.

Fig. 22. Classification results: (a), (b) authorized truck; (c), (d).

5   Conclusion

Throughout this paper, a Visual based method for Intruder vehicle Detection called "VID" is proposed in order to detect any unintended vehicle entering the platoon gap during the join maneuver. This method includes three main steps:

- ROI extraction by extracting the road area based on color feature.
- Vehicle detection based on Haar-like features and AdaBoost classifier.
- Vehicle classification based on the logo situated on the rear area of each truck using CNN.

We have analyzed the performance of "VID" in different weather conditions (sunny, cloudy, rainy). The results showed that "VID" performed effectively in good weather conditions (sunny circumstances) and provided acceptable rates in overcast conditions (cloudy weather). However, in extreme weather (rain and snow), noise and false detection are possible. As future work, we want to explore the method's performance in the context of varying road conditions and lane marker distortions. Additionally, further experiments and improvements are needed to ascertain the effectiveness of our method on urban roads, where vehicle density is higher than on highways, and the risk of an unwanted vehicle entering the platoon gap is significant.

References

1. MacDonald, J.: Electric vehicles to be 35% of global new car sales by 2040. Bloomberg New Energy Finan. **25**(4) (2016)

2. Terruzzi, L., Colombo, R., Segata, M.: Poster: on the effects of cooperative platooning on traffic shock waves. In: 2017 IEEE Vehicular Networking Conference (VNC), pp. 37–38. IEEE (2017)
3. Chetouane, A., Mabrouk, S., Jemili, I., Mosbah, M.: A comparative study of vehicle detection methods in a video sequence. In: Jemili, I., Mosbah, M. (eds.) DiCES-N 2019. CCIS, vol. 1130, pp. 37–53. Springer, Cham (2020). https://doi.org/10.1007/978-3-030-40131-3_3
4. Abdallah, A., Jemili, I., Mabrouk, S., Mosbah, M.: Leveraging GPS data for vehicle maneuver detection. In: Krief, F., Aniss, H., Mendiboure, L., Chaumette, S., Berbineau, M. (eds.) Communication Technologies for Vehicles, Nets4Cars/Nets4Trains/Nets4Aircraft 2020. LNCS, vol. 12574, pp. 39–54. Springer, Cham (2020). https://doi.org/10.1007/978-3-030-66030-7_4
5. Ksouri, C., Jemili, I., Mosbah, M., Belghith, A.: Data gathering for internet of vehicles safety. In: 2018 14th International Wireless Communications & Mobile Computing Conference (IWCMC), pp. 904–909. IEEE (2018)
6. Ksouri, C., Jemili, I., Mosbah, M., Belghith, A.: A unified smart mobility system integrating terrestrial, aerial and marine intelligent vehicles. In: Krief, F., Aniss, H., Mendiboure, L., Chaumette, S., Berbineau, M. (eds.) Communication Technologies for Vehicles, Nets4Cars/Nets4Trains/Nets4Aircraft 2020. LNCS, vol. 12574, pp. 203–214. Springer, Cham (2020). https://doi.org/10.1007/978-3-030-66030-7_18
7. Chetouane, A., Mabrouk, S., Jemili, I., Mosbah, M.: Vision-based vehicle detection for road traffic congestion classification. Concurrency Comput.: Pract. Exp. 34(7), e5983 (2022)
8. Bělinová, Z., Bureš, P., Jesty, P.: Intelligent transport system architecture different approaches and future trends. In: Duh, J., Hufnagl, H., Juritsch, E., Pfliegl, R., Schimany, H.K., Schonegger, H. (eds.) Data and Mobility: Transforming Information into Intelligent Traffic and Transportation Services, vol. 81, pp. 115–125. Springer, Berlin (2010). https://doi.org/10.1007/978-3-642-15503-1_11
9. Segata, M., Bloessl, B., Joerer, S., Dressler, F., Cigno, R.L.: Supporting platooning maneuvers through IVC: an initial protocol analysis for the JOIN maneuver. In: 2014 11th Annual Conference on Wireless On-demand Network Systems and Services (WONS), pp. 130–137. IEEE (2014)
10. Paranjothi, A., Atiquzzaman, M., Khan, M.S.: PMCD: platoon-merging approach for cooperative driving. Internet Technol. Lett. 3(1), e139 (2020)
11. Amoozadeh, M., Deng, H., Chuah, C.N., Zhang, H.M., Ghosal, D.: Platoon management with cooperative adaptive cruise control enabled by VANET. Veh. Commun. 2(2), 110–123 (2015)
12. Ploeg, J., et al.: Cooperative automated maneuvering at the 2016 grand cooperative driving challenge. IEEE Trans. Intell. Transp. Syst. 19(4), 1213–1226 (2017)
13. Huang, Z., Chu, D., Wu, C., He, Y.: Path planning and cooperative control for automated vehicle platoon using hybrid automata. IEEE Trans. Intell. Transp. Syst. 20(3), 959–974 (2018)
14. Rosique, F., Navarro, P.J., Fernández, C., Padilla, A.: A systematic review of perception system and simulators for autonomous vehicles research. Sensors 19(3), 648 (2019)
15. Peng, Y., Xu, M., Ni, Z., Jin, J.S., Luo, S.: Combining front vehicle detection with 3d pose estimation for a better driver assistance. Int. J. Adv. Rob. Syst. 9(3), 93 (2012)
16. Liu, Q., Li, Z., Yuan, S., Zhu, Y., Li, X.: Review on vehicle detection technology for unmanned ground vehicles. Sensors 21(4), 1354 (2021)

17. Sun, Z., Bebis, G., Miller, R.: On-road vehicle detection: a review. IEEE Trans. Pattern Anal. Mach. Intell. **28**(5), 694–711 (2006)
18. Wen, X., Zheng, Y.: An improved algorithm based on AdaBoost for vehicle recognition. In: the 2nd International Conference on Information Science and Engineering, pp. 981–984. IEEE (2010)
19. Nixon, M., Aguado, A.: Feature Extraction and Image Processing for Computer Vision. Academic press, Cambridge (2019)
20. Viola, P., Jones, M.J.: Robust real-time face detection. Int. J. Comput. Vision **57**, 137–154 (2004)
21. Shujuan, S., Zhize, X., Xingang, W., Guan, H., Wenqi, W., De, X.: Real-time vehicle detection using Haar-SURF mixed features and gentle AdaBoost classifier. In: the 27th Chinese Control and Decision Conference (2015 CCDC), pp. 1888–1894. IEEE (2015)
22. Papageorgiou, C.P., Oren, M., Poggio, T.: A general framework for object detection. In: Sixth International Conference on Computer Vision (IEEE Cat. No. 98CH36271), pp. 555–562. IEEE (1998)
23. Lienhart, R., Maydt, J.: An extended set of Haar-like features for rapid object detection. In: Proceedings of the International Conference on Image Processing, vol. 1. IEEE (2002)
24. Pavani, S.K., Delgado, D., Frangi, A.F.: Haar-like features with optimally weighted rectangles for rapid object detection. Pattern Recogn. **43**(1), 160–172 (2010)
25. Dalal, N., Triggs, B.: Histograms of oriented gradients for human detection. In: 2005 IEEE Computer Society Conference on Computer Vision and Pattern Recognition (CVPR 2005), vol. 1, pp. 886–893. IEEE (2005)
26. Ojala, T., Pietikäinen, M., Mäenpää, T.: Gray scale and rotation invariant texture classification with local binary patterns. In: Vernon, D. (ed.) ECCV 2000. LNCS, vol. 1842, pp. 404–420. Springer, Heidelberg (2000). https://doi.org/10.1007/3-540-45054-8_27
27. Lowe, D.G.: Distinctive image features from scale-invariant keypoints. Int. J. Comput. Vision **60**, 91–110 (2004)
28. Zhang, L., Chu, R., Xiang, S., Liao, S., Li, S.Z.: Face detection based on multiblock LBP representation. In: Lee, S.-W., Li, S.Z. (eds.) ICB 2007. LNCS, vol. 4642, pp. 11–18. Springer, Heidelberg (2007). https://doi.org/10.1007/978-3-540-74549-5_2
29. Rahman, M., Afrin, N.: Finding habitable exo planets using boosting algorithm (Doctoral dissertation, Brac University) (2018)
30. Vapnik, V.N.: The nature of statistical learning Theory (1995)
31. Overett, G., Petersson, L.: Large scale sign detection using HOG feature variants. In: 2011 IEEE Intelligent Vehicles Symposium (IV), pp. 326–331. IEEE (2011)
32. Li, D., Xu, L., Goodman, E.D., Xu, Y., Wu, Y.: Integrating a statistical background-foreground extraction algorithm and SVM classifier for pedestrian detection and tracking. Integr. Comput.-Aided Eng. **20**(3), 201–216 (2013)
33. Joshi, N., George, B., Vanajakshi, L.: Application of random forest algorithm to classify vehicles detected by a multiple inductive loop system. In: 2012 15th International IEEE Conference on Intelligent Transportation Systems, pp. 491–495. IEEE (2012)
34. Fukushima, K., Miyake, S., Ito, T.: Neocognitron: a neural network model for a mechanism of visual pattern recognition. IEEE Trans. Syst. Man Cybern. **5**, 826–834 (1983)

35. Jia, Y., et al.: Caffe: Convolutional architecture for fast feature embedding. In; Proceedings of the 22nd ACM International Conference on Multimedia, pp. 675–678 (2014)
36. Kim, J.: Automatic vehicle license plate extraction using region-based convolutional neural networks and morphological operations. Symmetry **11**(7), 882 (2019)
37. Hsu, S.C., Huang, C.L., Chuang, C.H.: Vehicle detection using simplified fast R-CNN. In: 2018 International Workshop on Advanced Image Technology (IWAIT), pp. 1–3. IEEE (2018)
38. Gharbi, H., Mabrouk, S.: ROI extraction for intrusion detection in platooning join maneuver. In: Jemili, I., Mosbah, M. (eds.) DiCES-N 2020. CCIS, vol. 1348, pp. 40–52. Springer, Cham (2020). https://doi.org/10.1007/978-3-030-65810-6_3
39. Jin, L.S., Wang, Y., Liu, J.H., Wang, Y.L., Zheng, Y.: Front vehicle detection based on Adaboost algorithm in daytime. J. Jilin Univ. (Eng. Technol. Edn.) **44**(6), 1604–1608 (2014)
40. Ying, C., Qi-Guang, M., Jia-Chen, L., Lin, G.: Advance and prospects of AdaBoost algorithm. Acta Automatica Sinica **39**(6), 745–758 (2013)
41. Kotu, V.: Model Evaluation in Data Science (ed. Kotu, V., Deshpande, B), pp. 263–279 (2019)
42. Kohavi, R., Provost, F.: Glossary of terms journal of machine learning. Mach. Learn. (1998)
43. Satzoda, R.K., Trivedi, M.M.: Multipart vehicle detection using symmetry-derived analysis and active learning. IEEE Trans. Intell. Transp. Syst. **17**(4), 926–937 (2015)
44. Gao, X., et al.: Selecting post-processing schemes for accurate detection of small objects in low-resolution wide-area aerial imagery. Remote Sens. **14**(2), 255 (2022)
45. Ibarra-Arenado, M., Tjahjadi, T., Pérez-Oria, J., Robla-Gómez, S., Jiménez-Avello, A.: Shadow-based vehicle detection in urban traffic. Sensors **17**(5), 975 (2017)
46. Tsai, L.W., Hsieh, J.W., Fan, K.C.: Vehicle detection using normalized color and edge map. IEEE Trans. Image Process. **16**(3), 850–864 (2007)
47. Chen, Y.L., Wu, B.F., Huang, H.Y., Fan, C.J.: A real-time vision system for nighttime vehicle detection and traffic surveillance. IEEE Trans. Ind. Electron. **58**(5), 2030–2044 (2010)
48. Jinying, H., Huizhen, H., Xiujin, L., Lijun, L.: Research on recognition of motional vehicle based on second-difference algorithm. In: 2009 IEEE International Symposium on Industrial Electronics (2009)
49. Chen, C., Zhang, X.: Moving vehicle detection based on union of three-frame difference. In: Jin, D., Lin, S. (eds.) Advances in Electronic Engineering, Communication and Management Vol.2. LNEE, vol. 140, pp. 459–464. Springer, Heidelberg (2012). https://doi.org/10.1007/978-3-642-27296-7_71
50. Li, W., Yao, J., Dong, T., Li, H., He, X.: Moving vehicle detection based on an improved interframe difference and a Gaussian model. In: 2015 8th International Congress on Image and Signal Processing (CISP), pp. 969–973. IEEE (2015)
51. Yang, H., Qu, S.: Real-time vehicle detection and counting in complex traffic scenes using background subtraction model with low-rank decomposition. IET Intel. Transp. Syst. **12**(1), 75–85 (2018)
52. Zhang, H., Wu, K.: A vehicle detection algorithm based on three-frame differencing and background subtraction. In: 2012 Fifth International Symposium on Computational Intelligence and Design, vol. 1, pp. 148–151. IEEE (2012)

114   H. Gharbi et al.

53. Garcia, F., Cerri, P., Broggi, A., de la Escalera, A., Armingol, J.M.: Data fusion for overtaking vehicle detection based on radar and optical flow. In: 2012 IEEE Intelligent Vehicles Symposium, pp. 494–499. IEEE (2012)
54. Lefebvre, S., Ambellouis, S.: Vehicle detection and tracking using mean shift segmentation on semi-dense disparity maps. In: 2012 IEEE Intelligent Vehicles Symposium, pp. 855–860. IEEE (2012)
55. Chen, L., Fan, L., Xie, G., Huang, K., Nüchter, A.: Moving-object detection from consecutive stereo pairs using slanted plane smoothing. IEEE Trans. Intell. Transp. Syst. **18**(11), 3093–3102 (2017)
56. Königshof, H., Salscheider, N.O., Stiller, C.: Realtime 3d object detection for automated driving using stereo vision and semantic information. In: 2019 IEEE Intelligent Transportation Systems Conference (ITSC), pp. 1405–1410. IEEE (2019)
57. Wongsaree, P., Sinchai, S., Wardkein, P., Koseeyaporn, J.: Distance detection technique using enhancing inverse perspective mapping. In: 2018 3rd International Conference on Computer and Communication Systems (ICCCS), pp. 217–221. IEEE (2018)
58. Kim, Y., Kum, D.: Deep learning based vehicle position and orientation estimation via inverse perspective mapping image. In: 2019 IEEE Intelligent Vehicles Symposium (IV), pp. 317–323. IEEE (2019)
59. Parodi, P., Piccioli, G.: A feature-based recognition scheme for traffic scenes. In: Proceedings of the Intelligent Vehicles 1995 Symposium, pp. 229–234. IEEE (1995)
60. Handmann, U., Kalinke, T., Tzomakas, C., Werner, M., Seelen, W.V.: An image processing system for driver assistance. Image Vis. Comput. **18**(5), 367–376 (2000)
61. Ito, T., Yamada, K., Nishioka, K.: Understanding driving situations using a network model. In: Proceedings of the Intelligent Vehicles 1995 Symposium, pp. 48–53. IEEE (1995)
62. Regensburger, U., Graefe, V.: Visual recognition of obstacles on roads. In: Proceedings of IEEE/RSJ International Conference on Intelligent Robots and Systems (IROS 1994), vol. 2, pp. 980–987. IEEE (1994)
63. Graefe, V., Efenberger, W.: A novel approach for the detection of vehicles on freeways by real-time vision. In: Proceedings of Conference on Intelligent Vehicles, pp. 363–368. IEEE (1996)
64. Cucchiara, R., Piccardi, M.: Vehicle detection under day and night illumination. In: IIA/SOCO (1999)
65. Bensrhair, A., Bertozzi, M., Broggi, A., Miche, P., Mousset, S., Toulminet, G.: A cooperative approach to vision-based vehicle detection. In: Proceedings 2001 IEEE Intelligent Transportation Systems, ITSC 2001, (Cat. No. 01TH8585), pp. 207–212. IEEE (2001)
66. Wu, J., Zhang, X.: A PCA classifier and its application in vehicle detection. In: Proceedings of the International Joint Conference on Neural Networks IJCNN 2001, (Cat. No. 01CH37222), vol. 1, pp. 600–604. IEEE (2001)
67. Matthews, N.D., An, P.E., Charnley, D., Harris, C.J.: Vehicle detection and recognition in greyscale imagery. Control. Eng. Pract. **4**(4), 473–479 (1996)
68. Papageorgiou, C., Poggio, T.: A trainable system for object detection. Int. J. Comput. Vision **38**, 15–33 (2000)
69. Sun, Z., Bebis, G., Miller, R.: Quantized wavelet features and support vector machines for on-road vehicle detection. In: 7th International Conference on Control, Automation, Robotics and Vision, 2002. ICARCV 2002, vol. 3, pp. 1641–1646. IEEE (2002)

70. Cheon, M., Lee, W., Yoon, C., Park, M.: Vision-based vehicle detection system with consideration of the detecting location. IEEE Trans. Intell. Transp. Syst. **13**(3), 1243–1252 (2012)
71. Lin, B.F., et al.: Integrating appearance and edge features for sedan vehicle detection in the blind-spot area. IEEE Trans. Intell. Transp. Syst. **13**(2), 737–747 (2012)

Securing Level Crossings with Edge Infrastructure and V2X Communications: A High-Performance Solution

Mayssa Dardour[1]($\boxtimes$), Hend Marouane[2], Mohamed Mosbah[1], Hassen Mnif[2], Toufik Ahmed[1], and Amel Meddeb-Makhlouf[2]

[1] Univ. Bordeaux, Bordeaux INP, CNRS, LaBRI, UMR5800, 33400 Talence, France
{mayssa.dardour,mosbah,tad}@labri.fr
[2] National School of Electronics and Telecommunications (ENET'Com), Sfax, Tunisia
{hend.marouane,hassene.mnif,amel.makhlouf}@enetcom.usf.tn

Abstract. The Internet of Vehicles (IoV) relies heavily on Vehicle-to-Everything (V2X) communications to enhance traffic safety and reduce the risk of accidents. This is particularly critical in level crossing scenarios where rail communications rely on their own infrastructure with unique access technology and message types. Solutions for safer level crossings need to be practical and suitable for implementation. In response, researchers have proposed Edge computing solutions, an IT architecture that processes data locally at the network's edge rather than in a central data center. This approach allows for real-time analysis of extensive data generated by connected devices. In this paper, we present a novel Edge computing infrastructure for safer level crossings, leveraging Cooperative Awareness Message (CAM) and Decentralized Environmental Notification Message (DENM) exchanges to identify hazardous situations. Our proposed solution integrates Intelligent Transport Systems (ITS) G5 and cellular 4G/5G V2X communication, optimized by a new algorithm for managing road-rail infrastructure in the Edge node. Our algorithm ensures Quality of Service (QoS) for V2X communications and enables road operators to prevent level crossing accidents. We demonstrate the effectiveness of our approach through simulations of different use cases and scenarios using OMNET++, SUMO, and Unity 3D.

Keywords: CAM · DENM · Edge Computing · IoV · ITS G5 · Level Crossing · QoS · V2X

1 Introduction

To lower the danger of accidents, Intelligent Transport Systems (ITS) utilize new technologies for vehicular communications. The primary goal is to offer effective solutions to increase road safety, particularly in railroad contexts. Several ITS stations enabling Vehicle to Everything (V2X) communications; such as Vehicle to Infrastructure (V2I), Vehicle to Vehicle (V2V), and Vehicle to Pedestrian (V2P) aim to exchange traffic data, to avert hazardous circumstances [1]. By giving rail and road users real-time traffic

I. Jemili et al. (Eds.): DiCES-N 2023, CCIS 2041, pp. 116–130, 2024.
https://doi.org/10.1007/978-3-031-52823-1_6

information, a well-designed intelligent level crossing system presents good chances to boost security and safety. Dedicated Short-Range Communications (DSRC) are valued as appealing options for supporting V2X connections. Numerous use cases can be examined in this context, especially when a train is considered in the Internet of Vehicles (IoV) paradigm. For the sake of safety, it is possible to implement advanced algorithms to ensure real-time communications between the various environment's entities like LIght Detection And Ranging (LIDAR), vehicles, pedestrians, Edge nodes, trains, etc. Such algorithms must ensure alert dissemination when dangerous circumstances are identified. Under normal traffic conditions, connected vehicles send periodic messages called Cooperative Awareness Messages (CAM). The CAM frequency is suggested to be a multiple of 100 ms and does not exceed 1s [2]. However, Decentralized Environmental Notification Messages (DENM) are transmitted when the objective is to send alerts and urgent information. There are four distinct types of DENM: (1) the announcement of a new alert uses a New DENM, (2) events can be updated by an Update DENM, (3) canceled by a Cancellation DENM, and (4) negated by using a Negation DENM [3]. Along these lines, the Edge node is proposed in this paper to manage CAM and DENM messages' transmission efficiently based on our proposed algorithm while considering delay requirements. Therefore, the adopted architecture allows our system's actors to communicate with the level crossing's infrastructure while ensuring real-time transmissions.

Through this work, we present an architecture for CAM and DENM transmissions in the level crossing area, as well as an algorithm for handling CAMs and DENMs when an unusual event occurs. We also propose a priority order for the alerts' generation following the event's severity. Then, we demonstrate a method that enables the train to brake before arriving at the level crossing when an emergency occurs. The proposed solution is based on hybrid ITS-G5/LTE 4G communications. Additionally, we highlight the significance of the Edge's role by comparing the Edge-based infrastructure to a cloud-based architecture while evaluating the Quality of Service (QoS) requirements.

The remainder of this paper is organized as follows. Section 2 discusses the solutions suggested in the reviews of related works. Section 3 introduces the chosen architecture. Section 4 explains the proposed algorithm. Several use cases are detailed in Sect. 5. Section 6 presents the performance evaluation and the simulation results. Finally, conclusion and future works are drawn in Sect. 7.

2 Related Works

The key points covered in this article have been discussed in research papers such as:

Francesco Romeo et al. [4] have analyzed the DENM performance on the 5G-V2X sidelink within the resource allocation scheme. This strategy based on message repetitions improves the DENM performance by using Maximum Ratio Combining (MRC) at the receiver with a negligible impact on periodic CAMs. This approach does not provide means to prioritize DENM types. Message classification and precision have not been taken into account. The simulated system is very limited and the specific case of the level crossing is not considered.

Zdenek Lokaj et al. [5] have proved that when traffic flow increases in city zones, the information sent to a driver via CAMs and DENMs has a considerable benefit. This work provides a model of a Cooperative (C)-ITS system that can make traffic safer. The limitation of this study is that it focuses on general V2X communications, so the authors did not consider a specific messaging strategy. Besides, they do not specify how to resume regular traffic conditions upon an emergency resolution. No alternative solutions are proposed for traffic congestion or collisions.

Erik de Britto e Silva et al. [6] have researched reinforcing traffic safety using CAM to verify velocity accuracy. They proposed using a Road Side Unit (RSU) equipped with a speed detection device to enforce the accuracy of the disseminated velocity. The RSU receives C-ITS messages and sends warning notifications (DENMs) when received information is inaccurate. This approach focuses only on sending alerts when the allowed vehicle's speed is exceeded. In addition, the exchange of messages between several RSUs is not mentioned.

Nagore Iturbe-Olleta et al. [7] have detailed the deployment of an ITS-G5 application based on analyzing CAM and DENM transmissions. They considered the management of alerts generated in a traffic control center by converting them to the corresponding DENMs and sending them to the specific RSU. For all studied scenarios, no train or level crossing are mentioned. Also, no priority assignment is considered on the 802.11p channel for the four DENM types (New, Update, Cancellation, and Negation).

3   Adopted Architecture

The new aspect of our chosen approach is the implementation of a level crossing infrastructure that ensures the exchange of information in real-time, as shown in Fig. 1.

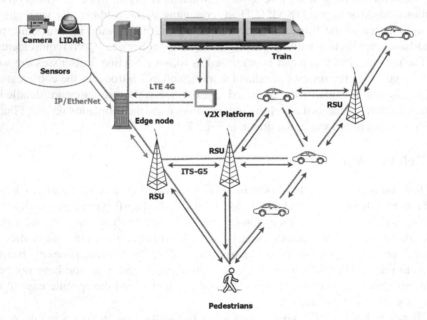

Fig. 1. Proposed architecture.

Many communications are supported to manage the exchange of messages under this architecture. An alert is sent to the Edge node when the LIDAR (or the camera, or another particular sensor) identifies an emergency. The Edge node transmits the received warning to the RSU. It should be noted that the Edge is mounted next to the RSU close to the level crossing to avoid high installation costs. We assume that its installation, next to the RSU, can provide advanced computing capabilities for processing and analyzing data locally at the network's edge, which is crucial for optimizing communication between vehicles and infrastructure and managing road-rail infrastructure. Consequently, it can be viewed as a higher-level computing platform that facilitates communication and data processing between RSUs and other connected devices, rather than as a standalone RSU. Through the V2X platform, the Edge node may also communicate with the train to alert it to emergencies. Assuming that the considered 500 m-zone supports 802.11p ITS-G5 communications [8], the RSU broadcasts the warning announcing the emergency case by sending a DENM to the nearby connected road users (The adopted DENM size for the realized simulations is equal to 300 bytes [9]). The CAM size is equivalent to 500 bytes [2].

Initially, CAM messages are exchanged periodically between the various environment components. Still, if an unusual circumstance arises, the CAMs are transmitted with a less priority order φ_n allowing the DENMs to have the highest priority order φ_0 on the 802.11p channel [10].

The Edge employs a method based on priority assignment to manage all DENM types, including New, Update, Cancellation, and Negation. The following section provides more information about the suggested algorithm.

4 Proposed Algorithm

A strategy for assigning messages in real-time systems in accordance with their priority is demonstrated in Algorithm 1.

Algorithm 1 Generation of messages at the Edge node

Input: $\eta^{[d]}$, $\zeta^{[c]}$
Output: $\{\tilde{N}_d\}^{[\eta[d]]}$, $\{\ddot{U}_d\}^{[\eta[d]]}$, $\{\c{C}_d\}^{[\eta[d]]}$, $\{\theta_{(neg)d}\}^{[\eta[d]]}$
Initialize: $i_{\eta[d]} \leftarrow 0$, $k_{\zeta[c]} \leftarrow 0$;

1 **while** $\check{T}_0 <= \check{T}_{nf}$ **do**
2   Broadcast $\zeta^{[c]}$; //every 100 ms
3      $k_{\zeta[c]} = k_{\zeta[c]} + 1$;
4   **if** (($\eta^{[d]}$ is detected) and ($\eta^{[d]} == \{\tilde{N}_d\}^{[\eta[d]]}$)) **then**
5   **if** (($\check{S}_{\text{å}} == Ł$) and ($\check{S}_{\text{å}} == \check{S}_{RS}$)) **then**
6   Broadcast $\eta^{[d]}$ with φ_0 ;
7              $i_{\eta[d]} \leftarrow i_{\eta[d]} + 1$;
8   **end if**
9   **else if** (($\eta^{[d]}$ is detected) and (($\eta^{[d]} == \{\ddot{U}_d\}^{[\eta[d]]}$) or ($\eta^{[d]} == \{\c{C}_d\}^{[\eta[d]]}$))) **then**
10   **if** ($\check{S}_{\text{å}} == \check{S}_{f\text{å}}$) **then**
11   Broadcast $\eta^{[d]}$ with φ_0 ;
12              $i_{\eta[d]} \leftarrow i_{\eta[d]} + 1$;
13   **else**
14   Ignore $\eta^{[d]}$;
15   **end if**
16   **else if** (($\eta^{[d]}$ is detected) and ($\eta^{[d]} == \{\theta_{(neg)d}\}^{[\eta[d]]}$)) **then**
17   **if** ($\check{S}_{\text{å}} != \check{S}_{f\text{å}}$) **then**
18   **if** (($\check{S}_{\text{å}} == Ł$) and ($\check{S}_{\text{å}} == \check{S}_{RS}$)) **then**
19   Broadcast $\eta^{[d]}$ with φ_0 ;
20                  $i_{\eta[d]} \leftarrow i_{\eta[d]} + 1$;
21   **end if**
22   **end if**
23   **end if**
        //Keep exchanging $\zeta^{[c]}$ in case of detection or not of $\eta^{[d]}$
        //Accord a lower priority order $[\varphi_{0+[1..n]}]$ to $\zeta^{[c]}$ when any $\eta^{[d]}$ ($\{\tilde{N}_d\}^{[\eta[d]]}$, $\{\ddot{U}_d\}^{[\eta[d]]}$, $\{\c{C}_d\}^{[\eta[d]]}$, $\{\theta_{(neg)d}\}^{[\eta[d]]}$) is being transmitted on the 801.11p channel.
24 **end while**
25 **End.**

Our approach is predicated on the understanding of unique parameters including: Source of the alert ($\check{S}_{\text{å}}$) (a LIDAR ($Ł$)), source of the first alert ($\check{S}_{f\text{å}}$), several recognized sources ($\check{S}_{RS}$), DENM ($\eta^{[d]}$) detection, and some specifications of each treated use-case. The following is the recommended hierarchy of relevance for the various DENM types: The new DENM ($\{\tilde{N}_d\}^{[\eta[d]]}$) has the highest priority, followed by the update DENM ($\{\ddot{U}_d\}^{[\eta[d]]}$), the cancellation DENM ($\{\c{C}_d\}^{[\eta[d]]}$) and the negation DENM ($\{\theta_{(neg)d}\}^{[\eta[d]]}$) respectively. We suppose that only the periodic exchange of CAMs ($\zeta^{[c]}$) is observed and that the number of exchanged CAMs increases every 100 ms ($k_{\zeta[c]} = k_{\zeta[c]} + 1$), but when an emergency is detected, an alert must be broadcasted ($i_{\eta[d]} \leftarrow i_{\eta[d]} + 1$) as long as the simulation is still running ($\check{T}_0 < = \check{T}_{nf}$).

Next, we provide a step-by-step description of each DENM type's generation strategy.

4.1 Generation of a New DENM

Once an emergency is identified, $\{\tilde{N}_d\}^{[\eta[d]]}$ is generated at the Edge node. We consider that an event detected by the infrastructure (Ł) has always the priority φ_0 for the proposed approach. We assume that if the same alert is triggered by more than one source ($\check{S}_{RS}$) then it is a major priority compared to an alert triggered by just one source. For the announced cases, the Edge node is informed that the problem persists. Consequently, it broadcasts the corresponding new DENM, otherwise, if unidentified sources have sent the emergency notification, the Edge decides that the regular periodic CAM exchange must not be interrupted, so no DENM message is generated.

4.2 Generation of an Update DENM

In some instances, the unexpected occurrence continues after broadcasting the new DENM with just minor adjustments to its position, severity, priority order, or other specifications. The Edge node, in this case, disseminates an update DENM to notify road users of these changes. If the $\{\ddot{U}_d\}^{[\eta[d]]}$ is produced by the same identifiable source as the original DENM ($\check{S}_{\ddot{a}} \leftarrow \check{S}_{f\ddot{a}}$), then it is broadcasted to road users. Otherwise, it is disregarded, preserving the first $\{\tilde{N}_d\}^{[\eta[d]]}$ on the 802.11p channel and the periodic exchange of $\zeta^{[c]}$ until the end of the simulation time (T $\leftarrow \check{T}_{nf}$). This type of DENM is delivered only when it becomes necessary to update the characteristics of the first broadcasted warning.

4.3 Generation of a Cancellation DENM

When the Edge is transmitting a $\{\tilde{N}_d\}^{[\eta[d]]}$ or a $\{\ddot{U}_d\}^{[\eta[d]]}$ and the emergency is resolved, it stops issuing the alert to disseminate a $\{\zeta_d\}^{[\eta[d]]}$. So, the priority accorded to the cancellation DENM is lower than the new and updated ones. The Edge node checks if the source that has originally issued the initial warning notification ($\eta^{[d]}$) when the abnormal event took place is also the transmitter of the cancellation notification ($\check{S}_{\ddot{a}} \leftarrow \check{S}_{f\ddot{a}}$). If the source is the same, then the $\{\zeta_d\}^{[\eta[d]]}$ is sent, and all traffic users realize that the problem is resolved. Suppose a different source broadcasts the cancellation DENM, the Edge dismisses it. In this case, the exchange of the $\{\tilde{N}_d\}^{[\eta[d]]}$ or the $\{\ddot{U}_d\}^{[\eta[d]]}$ persists along with the regular exchange of CAMs ($\zeta^{[c]}$) in the considered IoV environment.

4.4 Generation of a Negation DENM

It occasionally happens that the Edge receives a false alert while exchanging messages with other system actors during the various scenarios that could occur. In this circumstance, it instantly broadcasts a Negation DENM ($\{\theta_{(neg)d}\}^{[\eta[d]]}$) to inform road users that they shouldn't consider the erroneous warning. This kind of message must be generated by a station different from the original ($\check{S}_{\ddot{a}} \neq \check{S}_{f\ddot{a}}$) [11]. In this instance, when the LIDAR (Ł) and several recognized sources ($\check{S}_{RS}$) send this type of alert, it is broadcasted by the Edge. In fact, we grant the infrastructure (Ł) a high degree of confidentiality for our proposed process to avoid making decisions based on inaccurate information. It is crucial to mention that the $\{\theta_{(neg)d}\}^{[\eta[d]]}$ has the lowest priority order compared to other DENM messages.

4.5   Prioritization of Similar DENM Types

When the Edge receives $2 \times \eta^{[d]}$ of the same type according to the four classifications listed above, it categorizes them on the 802.11p channel based on the severity of the event they are reporting.

Then, it generates the DENM of the most dangerous event first, due to the DENM CauseCode field that gives information about the cause of the emergency (e.g., Accident, Roadworks, Vehicle breakdown, Human problem, collision risk, etc.). The DENM message includes a priority information field where the values 0 and 7 represent the highest and lowest priorities, respectively [12].

5   Use Cases

Different use-case analyses are carried out to validate the defined strategy. The selection of the studied use cases was carefully made based on their relevance to the current state-of-the-art in level crossing safety, as well as their representativeness of various scenarios and traffic conditions, ensuring that the proposed approach can be validated with high confidence and applicability.

5.1   Malfunction Detection

In this instance, a defect is discovered by a LIDAR (or a road user) at a distance $d = 10$m from the level crossing, typically connected to the lengthy duration of the barrier closure $T > 22$ s. At this point, the LIDAR alerts the Edge node, which then emits a DENM warning other road users of this special circumstance, as shown in Fig. 2. Some of them will decide to adjust their course to avoid any accident risk after receiving such a signal. Others will stop and wait to hear from the Edge, via DENM, that the unusual event has been canceled (By receiving a cancellation DENM from the source that first reported the issue, the Edge realizes that the problem has been fixed).

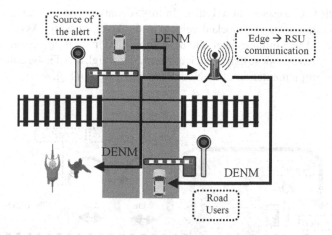

Fig. 2. Dissemination of barriers malfunction alert.

5.2 Detection of a Blocked Vehicle

Numerous eventualities are taken into account in this context and are handled in simulations:

Detection Without the Presence of a Train. In this scenario, the LIDAR detects a blocked vehicle on the railway and sends an alert to the Edge as shown in Fig. 3. (Barriers are opened and there is no coming train).

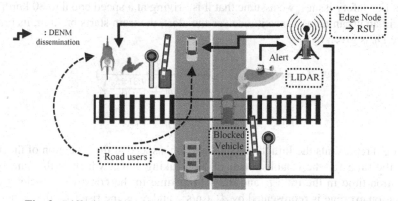

Fig. 3. Diffusion of the blocked vehicle alert with the absence of the train.

The Edge node transmits the warning received from the LIDAR at $T_{max} = t + 1s$ (maximum time for information processing). Once the Edge issues the DENM for problem resolution, regular traffic is resumed. As a result, some drivers will choose to use a different route. Others will pause and wait for an Edge DENM cancellation.

Detection with the Presence of a Train. In this scenario, a pedestrian, a vehicle or a LIDAR detects that there is a blocked vehicle at the level crossing. Assuming that the barriers are closed five minutes later, the train should be five kilometers away from the level crossing. So, we propose that it receives the alert through an LTE 4G communication and this, by the implementation of 2 eNodeBs as presented in Fig. 4.

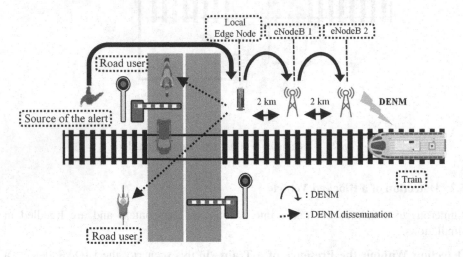

Fig. 4. Distribution of the blocked vehicle alert with the presence of the train.

In our trials, we suppose that the train receives the alert 5 min before the barriers closure. For safety issues, we assume that it is driving at a speed equal to 80 km/h (It is current in an urban area). Once it receives the alert, the train starts braking, its braking distance D_b is given by:

$$D_b = I_s \times (t_{p+e} + \frac{I_s}{2 \times \left(d_m \pm \frac{9.81 \times S_p}{10^3}\right)}) \tag{1}$$

$$\text{where} \quad t_{p+e} = t_p + t_e, t_p > 0, t_e > 0 \tag{2}$$

I_s (m/s) represents the Initial Speed (The train's speed at the reception of the alert), t_{p+e} is the time for the establishment of the braking force, which is the sum of the propagation time in the train t_p and the setting time in the convoy's vehicles t_e. The deceleration average is represented by d_m (m/s²) and S_p is the rise (‰) that is negative only in descent.

The graph in Fig. 5 illustrates the calculated distances of braking based on the DE-OCF diagrams of the brakes' evaluation [13]. Next, we will refer to this method as T1. Hence, Fig. 6 shows a comparison between the values obtained in Fig. 5 and the calculated distances for the train's braking obtained using (1), this method will have T2 as a reference in the next paragraph.

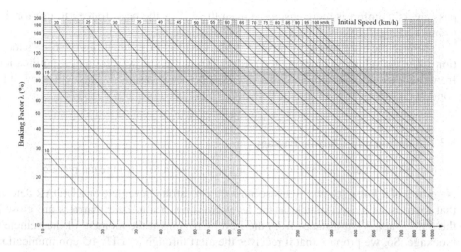

Fig. 5. Calculated distances of braking based on the evaluation of brakes' diagrams DE-OCF (T1) [13].

Keen-eyed observers will notice that for a braking factor $\lambda = 100\%$ and for a speed equal to 80 km/h, the train needs 254,16 m to brake, according to T1. However, it needs 270,8 m to stop, according to T2.

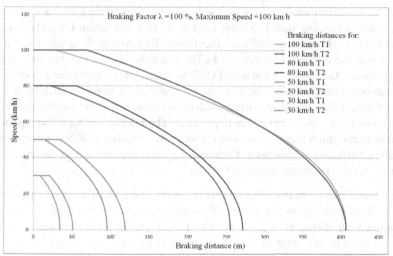

Fig. 6. Comparison between the Braking distances obtained based on T1 and T2 [14].

It is worth mentioning that the train needs to be alerted in advance to be able to brake safely (In our scenario, it receives the warning notification at the moment of the vehicle's blockage, and it starts to brake 5 km before barriers are closed). Since the train is a passengers' train, as the Braking distance increases (even by some meters), the passengers' comfort is more ensured. Given this, T2 is the best strategy to use for the train's braking.

Through the exchange of recurring CAMs, the local Edge identifies the train's location when the vehicle is blocking the railway. The train will wait for a new notification from the Edge node informing it that the issue has been resolved. This will allow it to continue traveling and prevent the collision.

5.3 Detection of a Chicane Passage

Several possibilities, such as the following, can be seen for the chicane passage:

Negation of a False Alert. In this scenario, a pedestrian, a vehicle or a LIDAR detects that there is a blocked vehicle at the level crossing. 5 min later, barriers are closed, the train is at a 5 km-distance from the Level Crossing at the moment of the vehicle's blockage. So, we propose that it receives the alert through an LTE 4G communication and this, by the implementation of 2 eNodeBs as presented in Fig. 4.

The sources of the alert in this instance—both the LIDAR and the pedestrian—are chosen to be at a distance $d_{1 \rightarrow max} = 10$ to 25 m from the Level Crossing (to ensure real-time alert transmission and ensure the QoS exigencies). They both send a DENM to the Edge after spotting a car making a chicane passage at the level crossing. The Edge node (assuming that the barriers are closed and that a train is approaching at a distance of $d_{tr} = 200$ m from the level crossing) broadcasts the alert at T_{max} $(t + 1s)$. In order to avoid further delay, another vehicle also tries to pass into a chicane. This vehicle sends a warning signal to other road users (a cancellation DENM) stating that the road is open. Having received the cancellation DENM, the Edge identifies that it is a false alert at the moment of reception T_RTR, since the vehicle that has just issued the warning was not the source of the initial DENM. Therefore, it lacks the authority to end the exceptional circumstance. The Edge node broadcasts a negation DENM as a result. To decrease the risk of accidents, drivers will either move away and modify their route or stop and wait for a subsequent signal to proceed. Then, when $t = \delta_{pr}$ (Corresponding to the problem resolution time), those who chose to wait receive a DENM informing them that the level crossing is now open. Consequently, automobiles and pedestrians resume their customary periodic exchange of CAMs.

Giving More Priority to the Infrastructure. Here, the pedestrian, the vehicle $\tilde{V}_2$, and the LIDAR all pick up on the vehicle $\tilde{V}_1$'s chicane passage. Sources of the warning notification are at distances $d_{1 \rightarrow max} = 10$ to 35 m from the level crossing. The barriers are closed and a train is approaching the level crossing (at $d_{tr} = 150$ m).

Actually, all of the three mentioned entities will communicate the emergency to the Edge via a DENM. As a result, the latter alerts other road users to unexpected event. Given that $\tilde{V}_1$ succeeds its chicane passage, $\tilde{V}_2$ tries to follow the chicane passage of $\tilde{V}_1$. It starts to move forward after broadcasting a fake signal in order to indicate that the level crossing is open. Given that the Edge prioritizes infrastructure and since the LIDAR is a key source of the first distributed DENM, a cancellation DENM must be sent by the LIDAR to terminate the DENM (unless a technical failure occurs, in which case the Edge will update its algorithms). Therefore, even if $\tilde{V}_2$ was one of the initial sources of the DENM, the urgency still exists for the Edge as long as the LIDAR is operational and has not yet cancelled the DENM. As a result, the Edge node broadcasts a negation DENM, as seen in Fig. 7.

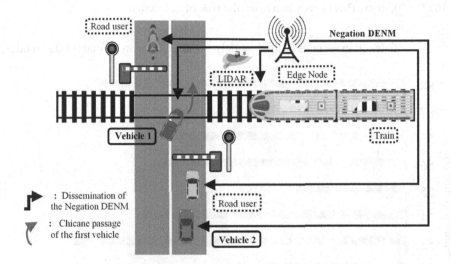

Fig. 7. Dissemination of the Negation DENM.

Road users must then wait for the barriers to reopen and for a new signal from the Edge before proceeding on their customary path.

6 Performance Evaluation and Simulation Results

Our approach is validated through simulations using OMNET++, SUMO Framework, and Unity 3D for the aforementioned use cases. Our primary objective is to demonstrate the effectiveness of the suggested approach. Despite differences in underlying characteristics among the use cases, our analysis reveals that there is no significant difference in performance or accuracy of the simulated scenarios. Thus, we conclude that the approach can be validated using any of the studied use cases with equal reliability.

By analyzing the results of our simulated "Detection of a blocked vehicle" scenario, we compare the performance of our architecture based on the Edge infrastructure to a central cloud-based architecture to demonstrate the effectiveness of our method. Furthermore, we sought to prove that the IoV paradigm we presented sends packets in real-time. In contrast to a central cloud-based messages exchange, Fig. 8 demonstrates that message latency for communications based on the Edge infrastructure is relatively low. For the sake of readability, in this comparison, we paid close attention to the simulation time points at which packets are being exchanged (there is no scale specified for the x-axis). The graph shows that, when considering Edge-based exchanges, the average latency is estimated to be very negligible. The time it takes to send packets is only a few microseconds (an average of 349,7254 µs), so real-time communication is guaranteed. This is significant in our case because we attempt to notify other road users of emergencies as soon as the abnormal event occurs. However, the graph in Fig. 8 demonstrates that cloud-based communications require a few milliseconds to initiate (An average of 2,465361807 ms). This latency increases the risk of accidents.

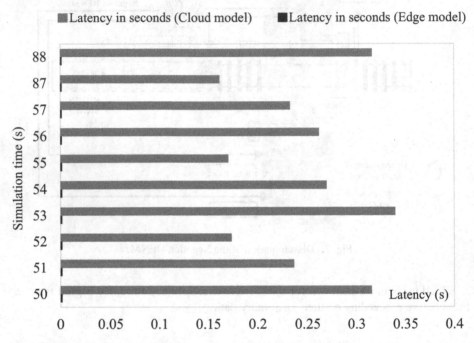

Fig. 8. Latency in a cloud-based architecture compared to an Edge-based infrastructure.

To further demonstrate the utility of our strategy, we examined the packet loss rates in both of the treated alternatives. This is shown in Fig. 9 where the average loss rate is very low (=3,4375%) for the Edge Infrastructure. Our simulations show that there is a significant difference between this packet loss rate and the corresponding value when a cloud infrastructure is considered, which ranges between 66,66% for the first sent packet and 16,16% for the last sent one (No scale is specified on the x-axis, we consider only the most relevant moments in the simulation time where packets are being exchanged).

These observations explain why we opted for an edge-based infrastructure to secure a level crossing area.

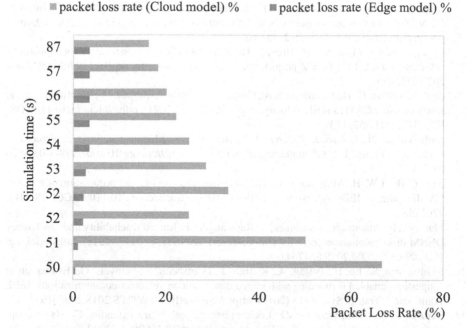

Fig. 9. Packet loss rate for both Edge-based and cloud-based models.

7 Conclusion and Future Works

This paper presents a new approach for managing DENMs and CAMs based on an Edge infrastructure at the level crossing. The key strategy is to declare dangerous use cases to avert serious accidents. The proposed architecture supports the interchange of all four DENM message types in the IoV environment. The transmissions are based on hybrid ITS G5/ LTE 4G communications. The simulated use cases demonstrate how the suggested approach could decrease accident risks in urban areas by satisfying real-time exchange requirements.

In future works, we plan to integrate the Radio Frequency Fingerprinting (RFF), a physical layer-based method for enhancing the security and privacy of transmitted information in order to fulfill the exchange confidentiality.

References

1. Wang, X., Mao, S., Gong, M.: An overview of 3GPP cellular vehicle-to-everything standards. GetMob.: Mob. Comput. Commun. **21**, 19–25 (2017). https://doi.org/10.1145/3161587.316 1593
2. Molina Masegosa, R., Sepulcre, M., Gozalvez, J., Berens, F., Martinez, V.: Empirical models for the realistic generation of cooperative awareness messages in vehicular networks. IEEE Trans. Veh. Technol. **69**(5), 5713–5717 (2020). https://doi.org/10.1109/TVT.2020.2979232
3. MacHardy, Z., Khan, A., Obana, K., Iwashina, S.: V2X access technologies: regulation, research, and remaining challenges. IEEE Commun. Surv. Tutor. 1 (2018). https://doi.org/10.1109/COMST.2018.2808444

4. Romeo, F., Campolo, C., Berthet, A.O., Molinaro, A.: Improving the DENM reliability over 5G-V2X sidelink through repetitions and diversity combining, pp. 352–357 (2021). https://doi.org/10.1109/5GWF52925.2021.00068

5. Lokaj, Z., Srotyr, M., Vanis, M., Broz, J.: Technical part of evaluation solution for cooperative vehicles within C-ROADS CZ project, pp. 1–5 (2020). https://doi.org/10.1109/SCSP49987.2020.9133885

6. de Britto e Silva, E., Hadiwardoyo, S.A., Costa, C.E., Marquez-Barja, J.M.: Reinforcing traffic safety by using CAM to verify velocity accuracy, pp. 1–8 (2021). https://doi.org/10.1109/DS-RT52167.2021.9576153

7. Iturbe-Olleta, N., Bilbao, J., Amengual, J., Brazalez, A., Mendizabal, J.: Deployment and simulation of a real ITS-G5 implementation (2021). https://doi.org/10.1007/978-3-030-926 84-7-3

8. Xie, Y., Ho, I.W.-H., Magsino, E.R.: The modeling and cross-layer optimization of 802.11p VANET unicast. IEEE Access 6, 171–186 (2018). https://doi.org/10.1109/ACCESS.2017.2761788

9. Marzouk, F., Alheiro, R., Rodriguez, J., Radwan, A.: Enhanced reachability and low latency DENM dissemination protocol for platoon-based VANETs, pp. 1–7 (2018). https://doi.org/10.1109/GLOCOM.2018.8647647

10. Kühlmorgen, S., Lu, H., Festag, A., Kenney, J., Gemsheim, S., Fettweis, G.: Evaluation of congestion- enabled forwarding with mixed data traffic in vehicular communications. IEEE Trans. Intell. Transp. Syst. 1–15 (2019). https://doi.org/10.1109/TITS.2018.2890619

11. Renzler, T., Stolz, M., Watzenig, D.: Looking into the path future: extending CAMs for cooperative event handling, pp. 1–5 (2020). https://doi.org/10.1109/VTC2020-Fall49728.2020.9348776

12. ETSI TS 102 637-2 V1.2.1. Intelligent Transport Systems (ITS); Vehicular Communications; Basic Set of Applications; Part 2: Specification of Cooperative Awareness Basic Service. Reference: RTS/ITS-0010018 (2011)

13. Implementing provisions on the Railways Ordinance - Dispositions d'exécution sur l'ordonnance sur les chemins de fer (DE-OCF). State as of July 1, 2016, DFETEC. Considering Article 81 of the Rail Road Ordinance of November 23, 1983 1) RS 742.141.1, (OFCL), 3003 Berne, n° of Article 802.650f

14. Kalbfuss, P.-Y.: Gestion du système ZBMS - calcul des courbes de freinage dynamiques des trains d'entreprises ferroviaires qui emploient un contrôle de la marche des trains conforme au standard ZBMS/Control of the ZBMS system - Calculation of the dynamic brake curves for trains operated by railway companies using a ZBMS-compliant train motion control system, Document number 21186. Landquart (2016)

A Formal Approach for a Railway Level Crossing Using the Event-B Method

Mohamed Tounsi[1,2]([✉]) and Faten Fakhfakh[1]

[1] ReDCAD Laboratory, ENIS, University of Sfax, Sfax, Tunisia
{mohamed.tounsi,faten.fakhfakh}@redcad.org
[2] College of Computer and Information Systems, Umm Al-Qura University,
Makkah, Saudi Arabia

Abstract. Accidents at level crossings often cause dramatic material and human damages that seriously affect the reputation of rail safety. Research on Level Crossing (LC) safety has attracted considerable attention in recent years. In this paper, we rely on formal methods, based on mathematical rigour, which provide real help for the designer to evaluate the behaviour of a system and avoid errors before its implementation. Thereby, we propose a railway LC system that suggests a new architecture which prevents very risky situations causing several accidents. To do so, we adopted the Event-B formal method to specify the safety requirements of our system and verify its correctness. Event-B is based on the refinement technique which allows a problem decomposition and then reduces modelling and verification effort.

Keywords: Railway · Level Crossing · Correctness · Formal methods · Event-B · Refinement

1 Introduction

Over the last decades, safety has been a major issue in railway operations. In particular, Level Crossing (LC) safety remains one of the most critical challenges that railway stakeholders need to handle. An LC is an intersection where a railway line intersects with a road or path at the same level. According to a statistical analysis of accidents at the European LC, there are more than 300 deaths every year in Europe [12]. Nevertheless, due to a complex operation context, and the lack of complete details about accidents, the risk assessment of LCs remains a challenging task. Therefore, LC safety in a railway field has to be urgently enhanced.

In order to guarantee the safety of such complex systems, scenario-based testing and simulation methods are far from being sufficient, since they do not ensure that systems behave correctly in all possible situations. However, adopting formal modeling has gained a great attention in the development of critical transport applications [5,6]. Formal methods are also desired by railway engineers thanks to the benefits and the potential of model-based engineering systems. In fact, these methods consist in expressing the system behaviour as mathematical formulas. They aim to specify the functionality of a system and provide an efficient way to prove its properties without worrying about the possible scenarios.

Therefore, the main purpose of our research is the use of formal methods to specify the safety requirements of LC systems. Our work enables to count the number of upcoming vehicles from the two sides of the LC. Indeed, it informs each vehicle when it can reach the LC. The main goal of the developed system is to guarantee a safe LC and a reliable passage of trains and vehicles. To do so, we adopted the Event-B formal method, which relies on a refinement-based model development. The refinement technique deals with the complexity of a system since it consists in introducing the different properties in a step-by-step fashion. Moreover, it is the main basis of the correct-by-construction approach [9].

The remainder of this paper will be divided into the following sections: In Sect. 2, we give a brief overview of the Event-B formal method and the correct-by-construction approach. In Sect. 3, we provide a description of our proposed railway LC system. Section 4 details our system formalization using the Event-B method. The related work is presented in Sect. 5. Finally, the last Sect. 6 concludes the paper and provides insights for future works.

2   Preliminaries

In this section, we introduce preliminary details about the Event-B formal method and the correct-by-construction approach which represent the essential concepts of our proposed formal development of the railway LC system.

2.1   Event-B Modeling Method

Event-B [1] is a formal method enabling the development of software through consecutive refinements. Its modeling language relies upon the first-order predicate logic and the set theory. Moreover, it uses two main structures to specify a software system: contexts and machines. The context specifies the static part of a model which may include carrier sets, constants, axioms, and theorems that can be derived from the axioms of a context. A context may be extended by another context to introduce more elements. A machine describes the dynamic elements of a system. It consists of several components: variables, invariants, theorems, and events. In fact, the variables express the different states of the system. Invariants define the properties of the variable that should always be maintained in each state. Theorems express the properties derivable from the invariants. Events specify the behavior of a system by modifying the set of variables. An event is fired when its guards are satisfied. The actions represent the result of an event execution. In order to use the static elements of the system, a machine may see one or more contexts.

2.2   Correct-by-Construction Approach

The correct-by-construction approach [9] aims to create a correct software. The foundation of this approach is the refinement technique. It is the main feature of Event-B as it enables to enrich a machine in a step-by-step manner. In the refined machine, new variables and events can be introduced. Furthermore, the abstract variables and events can be replaced by concrete ones. The relationship between the variables in the abstract and concrete model is expressed by gluing invariants.

To ensure the correctness of contexts, machines and the refinement process, we must validate a number of proof obligations (POs) which are automatically generated by the "RODIN" platform [2]. Some POs are related to the machine/-context elements while others are related to the refinement process. The POs enable checking whether the events preserve the invariants of the system and that all events are feasible. The definitions of all the PO types are clearly given in [1]. Moreover, the POs can be discharged either automatically by an integrated proof tool or through interactive proof steps.

3   Railway Level Crossing System

We present in Fig. 1 the overall process of our railway level crossing system. We assume that the traffic road crossing the railway is usually a one-way lane. We describe the different components of our system in Table 1.

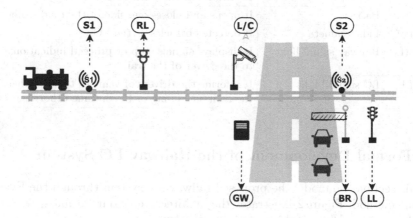

Fig. 1. The graphical representation of the LC system

For a better understanding, we suppose that the train comes from the left side. If the sensor S1 detects the train, it sends an approaching message to the GW. Here, we can distinguish two cases:

- **Case 1:** If the L/C detects an obstacle at the LC, it sends a message to the GW. This latter communicates with the RL to display a red signal. So, the train must stop.

- **Case 2:** If the RL displays a green signal, the train continues running. So, the sensor S1 detects the train and sends an approaching message to the GW. After that, the GW sends a message to the BR about closing the LC. Moreover, it informs the drivers of vehicles to stop by changing the signal of the LL to red. At this time, the train passes the LC safely and the other components remain as they are. Then, after crossing the railway, the sensor S2 sends a message to the GW to lift the BR. Therefore, in order to change the LL to green, it should be ensured that the number of cars after the LC does not exceed a certain number. This number is computed according to the distance covered by the gateway. In our work, we assume that only a single vehicle can cross the crossing level at a time.

Table 1. Description and role of each item of the proposed system

Item	Description	Role
GW	Level crossing control and Gateway	It connects LC components, communicates with vehicles and takes decisions about closing and reopening the LC
S1	Sensor	It detects the train and sends an approaching message to the GW
S2	Sensor	It detects the train and sends an exit message to the GW if the train exits the LC
BR	Barrier	It opens and closes one side of the road traffic
L/C	Lidar/camera	It detects obstacles at the LC
RL	Railway signal light	It displays signals stop or proceed indications to the driver of the train
LL	LC signal Light	It informs the drivers of vehicles to stop when the train is coming or to continue otherwise

4   Formal Development of the Railway LC System

In this section, we model the proposed railway LC system through the Event-B formal method. Figure 2 illustrates the architecture of our formal specification which consists of five machines and two contexts:

- The context "C0" encodes the railway and the road structure. The context "C1" extends "C0" and defines all labels of the system.
- The first machine "M0" specifies the main events performed by a train at the LC. It uses properties defined in the context "C1".
- The machine "M1" refines the first one. It adds events to encodes vehicle activities.
- The third machine "M2" refines "M1". It formalizes the railway signal light, lidar/camera, and LC signal light properties.

– The fourth machine "M3" refines "M2" to introduce local labels of vehicles.
– The last machine "M4" refines "M3" and specifies the vehicle numbering.

Due to lack of space, we present in this paper only the main elements of our formalization.

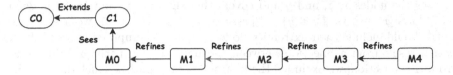

Fig. 2. The Event-B specification structure of the LC system

4.1   Formal Specification of the Context C0

The context C0 describes the static properties of the railway and the road (see Listing 1.1). They are represented by a simple, connected and oriented graph. They are specified by two paths. A path is a linear graph where nodes are listed in a defined order $(N_1, N_2, ..., N_n)$ and edges connect two neighbouring nodes (N_i, N_{i+1}) where $i \in \{1, 2, ...n - 1\}$. The intersection between the road and the railway paths is an edge representing the LC zone. To specify the railway and the road path, we start by defining a set of positions as given in Table 2.

Table 2. Description of the different positions in the railway and the road path

Positions	Description
s1 and s2	The positions of the sensor S1 and the sensor S2 respectively
rl	The position of the first railway light
cz0 and cz1	The positions of the beginning and the end of the crossing zone respectively
r0 [resp. r1]	The position of the first [resp. last] place covered by the gateway in the road before [resp. after] the crossing zone

In Fig. 3, we present a graphical representation of the railway and the road structure.

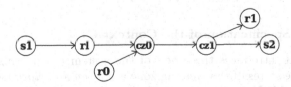

Fig. 3. Graphical representation of the railway and the road

Formally, a position is defined as a node (P is the position set) and an edge is specified as a link between two nodes ($axm1$). The axioms $axm2$ and $axm3$ respectively ensure that the graph is simple and directed. The domain restriction "$P \lhd id$" is a subset of the relation id which includes all the pairs whose first component is in P. In $axm4$, we define a path as a finite sequence of edges which joins two nodes. For example, a path between x and y which crosses the nodes x, z, and y and covers the edges (x, z) and (z, y) is defined as follows: $x \mapsto y \mapsto \{x, z, y\} \mapsto \{x \mapsto z, z \mapsto y\}$. In $axm5$, we assert that a path should include their extremity nodes. A path is composed of a set of edges which result from a bijection between the nodes of the path ($axm6$). In fact, from this bijection, we excluded the first node of the path x which does not have a predecessor node and the last node of the path y that does not have a successor node. Then, in $axm7$, we mentioned that a path is a connected graph, while in $axm8$ and $axm9$, we use the operator $partition$ to define instances of the sets P and $edges$. The $axm10$ [resp. $axm11$], defines the path $railway$ [resp. $road$] as a set of edges with respect to our use case.

Listing 1.1. Axioms of the context C0

```
axm1: edges ⊆ P × P
axm2: P ◁ id ∩ edges = ∅
axm3: edges ∩ edges⁻¹ = ∅
axm4: path ⊆ (P × P) × ℙ(P) × ℙ(edges)
axm5: ∀x, y, z, S·x ≠ y ∧ z ⊆ P ∧ S ∈ ℙ(edges) ∧ ((x ↦ y) ↦ z) ↦ S ∈ path
⇒ x ∈ z ∧ y ∈ z
axm6: ∀x, y, Z, S·x ≠ y ∧ Z ⊆ P ∧ S ∈ ℙ(edges) ∧
((x ↦ y) ↦ Z) ↦ S ∈ path ⇒ S ∈ Z \ {y} ⤖ Z \ {x}
axm7: ∀x, y, Z, S·x ≠ y ∧ Z ⊆ P ∧ S ∈ ℙ(edges) ∧
((x ↦ y) ↦ Z) ↦ S ∈ path ⇒ (∀q·q ⊆ Z ∧ y ∈ q ∧ S[q] ⊆ q ⇒ Z = q)
axm8: partition(P, {s1}, {s2}, {rl}, {cz0}, {cz1}, {r0}, {r1})
axm9: partition(edges, {s1 ↦ rl}, {rl ↦ cz0}, {cz0 ↦ cz1}, {cz1 ↦ r1},
{r0 ↦ cz0}, {cz1 ↦ s2})
axm10: railway = {s1 ↦ rl, rl ↦ cz0, cz0 ↦ cz1, cz1 ↦ s2}
axm11: road = {r0 ↦ cz0, cz0 ↦ cz1, cz1 ↦ r1}
```

Finally, we added the following theorems ($thm1$ and $thm2$) to prove that $railway$ and $road$ sets comply with the previously defined axioms through the following theorems:

- thm1 : $(r0 \mapsto r1) \mapsto \{r0, cz0, cz1, r1\} \mapsto road \in path$
- thm2 : $(s1 \mapsto s2) \mapsto \{s1, rl, cz0, cz1, s2\} \mapsto railway \in path$

4.2   Formal Specification of the Context C1

The C1 context introduces the labels of the system (see Listing 1.2). In fact, the two possible states of the crossing zone are: *open* and *close* (see $axm1$). The railway and road light signals are specified by the $axm2$ and $axm3$ respectively, while in $axm4$, we describe the possible states of the barrier: *up* and *down*.

We specify in $axm5$ the lidar states which can be $clear\_LC$ or not_clear_LC. As for $axm6$, it specifies the possible positions of a vehicle: away (very far), before, inside or just after the LC zone. In $axm7$, we define two constants: $max\_cars\_before\_LC$ and $max\_cars\_after\_LC$. We assume that the first one [resp. the second one] corresponds to the maximal number of vehicles in the path $(r0 \mapsto cz0)$ [resp. $(cz1 \mapsto r1)$] where a gateway can connect with them.

Listing 1.2. Axioms of the context C1

---

axm1: $partition(crossing\_states, \{open\}, \{close\})$
axm2: $partition(RL\_states, \{Green\}, \{Red\})$
axm3: $partition(Light\_state, \{red\}, \{no\_light\})$
axm4: $partition(BR\_states, \{up\}, \{down\})$
axm5: $partition(lidar\_states, \{clear\_LC\}, \{not\_clear\_LC\})$
axm6: $partition(vehicle\_position, \{away\_LC\}, \{before\_LC\}, \{inside\_LC\}, \{after\_LC\})$
axm7: $max\_cars\_before\_LC \in \mathbb{N}_1 \wedge max\_cars\_after\_LC \in \mathbb{N}_1$

4.3   Formal Specification of the Machine M0

The first machine, called M0, specifies the basic events of the model. This level is very abstract in which we can observe only four events:

- **Open_LC** occurs when the train leaves the LC zone. More precisely, the train moves from the $(cz0 \mapsto cz1)$ path to the $(cz1 \mapsto s2)$ path.
- **Close_LC** occurs when the train enters the first path of the railway $(s1 \mapsto rl)$.
- **move_inside_LC** occurs when the train moves forward from $(s1 \mapsto rl)$ or $(rl \mapsto cz0)$ to the next path.
- **move_away_LC** occurs when the train exits $(cz1 \mapsto s2)$ path and therefore it leaves the railway.

In this first machine, we define two variables: $crossing\_road\_state$ and $train\_inside$ (see Listing 1.3). The first variable represents the state of the crossing zone. It is "close" [resp. "open"] if vehicles cannot [resp. can] cross the railway (see inv1). The $train\_inside$ variable attributes the value "TRUE" [resp. "FALSE"] to a particular path of the railway if a train is [resp. is not] inside (see $inv2$). Through "$inv3$" and "$inv4$", we specify that the crossing zone is closed if there is a train inside $(s1 \mapsto rl)$ or $(rl \mapsto cz0)$ or $(cz0 \mapsto cz1)$ paths and open, otherwise. Then, the invariant "$inv5$" asserts that no more than one train can be present inside $(s1 \mapsto rl)$ or $(rl \mapsto cz0)$ or $(cz0 \mapsto cz1)$ paths.

Listing 1.3. Invariants of the machine M0

$inv1 : crossing\_road\_state \in \{cz0 \mapsto cz1\} \rightarrow crossing\_states$
$inv2 : train\_inside \in railway \rightarrow BOOL$
$inv3 : crossing\_road\_state(cz0 \mapsto cz1) = close \Leftrightarrow (\exists x, y \cdot x \mapsto y \subset$
    $railway \setminus \{cz1 \mapsto s2\} \wedge train\_inside(x \mapsto y) = TRUE)$
$inv4 : crossing\_road\_state(cz0 \mapsto cz1) = open \Leftrightarrow$
    $train\_inside[railway \setminus \{cz1 \mapsto s2\}] = \{FALSE\}$
$inv5 : \forall x, y \cdot x \mapsto y \in (railway \setminus \{cz1 \mapsto s2\}) \wedge train\_inside(x \mapsto y) = TRUE$
    $\Rightarrow train\_inside[railway \setminus \{cz1 \mapsto s2, x \mapsto y\}] = \{FALSE\}$

Because of the space limitation, we detailed only the events $Open\_LC$ and $Close\_LC$ of the M0 machine. The event $Open\_LC$ (see Listing 1.4) can be activated if the state of the crossing zone is equal to "$close$" and the train moves from the $(cz0 \mapsto cz1)$ path to the $(cz1 \mapsto s2)$ path. In the action component, the crossing zone state takes the state "$open$" and the train moves to the $(cz1 \mapsto s2)$ path.

Listing 1.4. Event $Open\_LC$, in M0

```
EVENT  Open_LC
WHEN
  grd1 : crossing_road_state(cz0 ↦ cz1) = close
  grd2 : train_inside(cz0 ↦ cz1) = TRUE
THEN
  act1 : crossing_road_state(cz0 ↦ cz1) := open
  act2 : train_inside := (train_inside \ {cz0 ↦ cz1 ↦ TRUE, cz1 ↦ s2 ↦ FALSE})
          ∪{cz1 ↦ s2 ↦ TRUE, cz0 ↦ cz1 ↦ FALSE}
END
```

The event $Close\_LC$ (see Listing 1.5) can be triggered if the state of the crossing zone is equal to $open$ and the train enters the first path of the railway $(s1 \mapsto rl)$. The actions defined in the clause "THEN" update the crossing zone state and the train is now in the first path of the railway $(s1 \mapsto rl)$.

Listing 1.5. Event $Close\_LC$, in M0

```
EVENT  Close_LC
WHEN
  grd1 : crossing_road_state(cz0 ↦ cz1) = open
THEN
  act1 : crossing_road_state(cz0 ↦ cz1) := close
  act2 : train_inside := (train_inside \ {s1 ↦ rl ↦ FALSE}) ∪ {s1 ↦ rl ↦ TRUE}
END
```

4.4 Formal Specification of the Machine M1

The second machine M1 refines the first one and adds new details to it (see Listing 1.6). At this level, we can observe the vehicle traffic. Formally, we define a new variable v_inside to specify the set of present vehicles at each path of the road (see $inv1$). Moreover, we restrict the number of vehicles in each road path by thresholds previously defined in the context (see $inv2$, $inv3$ and $inv4$). Through "$inv5$", we ensure that a vehicle crossing the rails will find a free place in the following path $(cz1 \mapsto r1)$. The invariant "$inv6$" asserts that no vehicles can be at two paths at the same time. Finally, when the crossing zone is closed then there is no vehicle inside the $(sz0 \mapsto cz1)$ $(inv7)$.

Listing 1.6. Invariants of the machine M1

$inv1 : v\_inside \in road \rightarrow \mathbb{P}(Cars)$
$inv2 : card(v\_inside(r0 \mapsto cz0)) \leq max\_cars\_before\_LC$
$inv3 : card(v\_inside(cz1 \mapsto r1)) \leq max\_cars\_after\_LC$
$inv4 : card(v\_inside(cz0 \mapsto cz1)) \leq 1$
$inv5 : card(v\_inside(cz0 \mapsto cz1)) = 1 \Rightarrow$
$\qquad card(v\_inside(cz1 \mapsto r1)) < max\_cars\_after\_LC$
$inv6 : \forall x, y, z, w \cdot x \mapsto y \in road \land z \mapsto w \in road \land x \mapsto y \neq z \mapsto w \Rightarrow$
$\qquad v\_inside(x \mapsto y) \cap v\_inside(z \mapsto w) = \varnothing$
$inv7 : crossing\_road\_state(cz0 \mapsto cz1) = close \Rightarrow v\_inside(cz0 \mapsto cz1) = \varnothing$

At this level, we reinforce the event $Close\_LC$ guard by adding a new condition $v\_inside(cz0 \mapsto cz1) = \varnothing$ to fulfill the invariant "$inv7$" property. Indeed, we have specified four new events to model the vehicular movement around the railway: $enter\_road$, $enter\_road\_LC$, $exit\_road\_LC$ and $exit\_road$.

The $enter\_road$ event (see Listing 1.7) is activated when a vehicle enters the $(r0 \mapsto cz0)$ path. In the guard component, we state in $grd1$ that the $vehicle$ belongs to the finite set of vehicles $Cars$. We assert that the $vehicle$ is not already on the road paths ($grd2$), but there is at least one free place in that path ($grd3$). Then, in the action component of this event, we added the vehicle to the set of vehicles which are in the $(r0 \mapsto cz0)$ path.

Listing 1.7. Event $enter\_road$, in M1

```
EVENT enter_road
ANY vehicule
WHEN
grd1 : vehicule ∈ Cars
grd2 : ∀CARS·CARS ∈ v_inside[road] ⇒ vehicule ∉ CARS
grd3 : card(v_inside(r0 ↦ cz0)) < max_cars_before_LC
THEN
  act1 : v_inside(r0 ↦ cz0) := v_inside(r0 ↦ cz0) ∪ {vehicule}
END
```

The Listing 1.8 presents the $enter\_road\_LC$ event which enables a vehicle to enter the crossing zone ($(cz0 \mapsto cz1)$ path). More precisely, a vehicle should be in the $(r0 \mapsto cz0)$ path (see $grd1$) and the crossing zone must be open (see $grd4$) and free (see $grd2$). Indeed, to ensure that the vehicle does not suck in the $(cz0 \mapsto cz1)$ path, we have to guarantee a free place in the $(cz1 \mapsto r1)$ path (see $grd2$). The action $act1$ uses the overriding operator "$\Leftarrow$" in Event-B to update the v_inside variable and therefore, the vehicle becomes inside the crossing zone.

Listing 1.8. Event $enter\_road\_LC$, in M1

```
EVENT enter_road_LC
ANY vehicule,X
WHEN
grd1 : vehicule ∈ v_inside(r0 ↦ cz0)
grd2 : v_inside(cz0 ↦ cz1) = ∅ ∧ card(v_inside(cz1 ↦ r1)) < max_cars_after_LC
grd3 : X = v_inside(r0 ↦ cz0)
grd4 : crossing_road_state(cz0 ↦ cz1) = open
THEN
  act1 : v_inside := v_inside ⇐
      {r0 ↦ cz0 ↦ (X \ {vehicule}), cz0 ↦ cz1 ↦ {vehicule}}
END
```

The Listing 1.9 presents the *exit_road_LC* event. The vehicle inside the crossing zone is moving and it becomes in the $(cz1 \mapsto r1)$ path.

Listing 1.9. Event *exit_road_LC*, in M1

```
EVENT exit_road_LC
ANY vehicule, X
WHEN
grd1 : v_inside(cz0 ↦ cz1) = {vehicule}
grd2 : X = v_inside(cz1 ↦ r1)
THEN
   act1 : v_inside := v_inside ◁ {cz1 ↦ r1 ↦ (X ∪ {vehicule}), cz0 ↦ cz1 ↦ ∅}
END
```

Finally, the *exit_road* event enables the vehicles to exit the $(cz1 \mapsto r1)$ path.

4.5 Formal Specification of the Machine M2

The third machine M2 refines M1 and adds five new variables: *open_lidar*, *road_light_state*, *Barrier_state*, *Lidar_states*, and *Railway_light_state*. These variables are detailed by the following invariants (see Listing 1.10). The five first invariants define these variables where BR is the barrier, LL is the light signal on the road side, *lidar* is the LC obstruction detector, and RL are the railway light signals. The invariant *inv6* asserts that all the railway light signals are synchronized: they are *Green* or *Red*. The barrier and the road light should be respectively *down* and *red* if the crossing zone is closed (see *inv7*). Likewise, the barrier and the road light should be respectively *up* and *no_light* if the crossing zone is open (see *inv8*). In invariant (*inv9*) [resp. (*inv10*)] we mention that the railway light signals are *Green* [resp. *Red*] when the crossing zone is clear [resp. not clear]. Through *inv11* and *inv12*, we precise that the lidar is activated only if the train is inside the $(rl \mapsto cz0)$ path.

Listing 1.10. Invariants of the machine M2

```
inv1 : Barrier_state ∈ {BR} → BR_states
inv2 : road_light_state ∈ {LL} → Light_state
inv3 : Lidar_states ∈ {lidar} → lidar_states
inv4 : Railway_light_state ∈ RL → RL_states
inv5 : open_lidar ∈ BOOL
inv6 : Railway_light_state[RL] = {Green} ∨ Railway_light_state[RL] = {Red}
inv7 : crossing_road_state(cz0 ↦ cz1) = close ⇒
       Barrier_state(BR) = down ∨ road_light_state(LL) = red
inv8 : crossing_road_state(cz0 ↦ cz1) = open ⇒
       Barrier_state(BR) = up ∨ road_light_state(LL) = no_light
inv9 : Lidar_states(lidar) = clear_LC ∧ train_inside(rl ↦ cz0) = TRUE ⇒
       Railway_light_state[RL] = {Green}
inv10 : Railway_light_state[RL] = {Red} ⇒
        Lidar_states(lidar) = not_clear_LC ∧ train_inside(rl ↦ cz0) = TRUE
inv11 : train_inside[railway \ {rl ↦ cz0}] = {TRUE} ⇒ open_lidar = FALSE
inv12 : open_lidar = TRUE ⇒ train_inside(rl ↦ cz0) = TRUE
```

At this level, we refine the events of the machine $M1$ and we add two new events: *detect_object* and *detect_no_object*. The *detect_object* event is triggered when there is an obstacle in the crossing zone. In this case, all railway light signals become *Red* (see Listing 1.11).

Listing 1.11. Event *detect_object*, in M2

```
EVENT  detect_object
WHEN
grd1 : open_lidar = TRUE
grd2 : Railway_light_state[RL] = {Green}
grd3 : Lidar_states(lidar) = clear_LC
THEN
  act1 : Railway_light_state := RL × {Red}
  act2 : Lidar_states(lidar) := not_clear_LC
END
```

The *detect_no_object* event is triggered when the obstacle is removed. Then, the railway light signals turn green and the train can cross the crossing zone level (see Listing 1.12).

Listing 1.12. Event *detect_no_object*, in M2

```
EVENT  detect_no_object
WHEN
grd1 : open_lidar = TRUE
grd2 : Railway_light_state[RL] = {Red}
grd3 : Lidar_states(lidar) = not_clear_LC
THEN
act1 : Railway_light_state := RL × {Green}
act2 : Lidar_states(lidar) := clear_LC
act3 : open_lidar := FALSE
END
```

The *move_inside_LC* is now replaced by two concrete events. The first one (*move_inside_LC*(1), see Listing 1.13) specifies the train movement from ($s1 \mapsto rl$) to ($rl \mapsto cz0$) paths. Furthermore, the gateway activates the Lidar to detect an object and may probably, in certain case, stop the train.

Listing 1.13. Event *move_inside_LC(1)*, in M2

```
EVENT  move_inside_LC(1)  REFINES  move_inside_LC
WHEN
grd1 : train_inside(s1 ↦ rl) = TRUE
grd2 : open_lidar = FALSE
THEN
act1 : train_inside := train_inside ⩤ {s1 ↦ rl ↦ FALSE, rl ↦ cz0 ↦ TRUE}
act2 : open_lidar := TRUE
END
```

The second event *move_inside_LC*(2) (see Listing 1.14) specifies the train's movement from ($rl \mapsto cz0$) to ($cz0 \mapsto cz1$) paths. This movement can be realized if the Lidar asserts that no obstacle is in the crossing zone.

Listing 1.14. Event *move_inside_LC(2)*, in M2

```
EVENT move_inside_LC(2) REFINES move_inside_LC
WHEN
grd1 : train_inside(rl ↦ cz0) = TRUE
grd2 : Lidar_states(lidar) = clear_LC
THEN
act1 : train_inside := train_inside ⩤ {rl ↦ cz0 ↦ FALSE, cz0 ↦ cz1 ↦ TRUE}
act2 : open_lidar := FALSE
END
```

4.6 Formal Specification of the Machine M3

At this level, we refine the machine M2. We add a new variable *v_position* to encode the vehicle position. This variable will replace the *v_inside* variable to make the position as local information for each vehicle. In Listing 1.15, we provide the invariants list of this machine. As for the *inv1*, it defines the new variable and while the other invariants specify all the different position cases. Finally, the events of this machine are refined by replacing *v_inside* with *v_position*.

Listing 1.15. Invariants of M3 machine

```
inv1 : v_position ∈ Cars → vehicule_position
inv2 : dom(v_position ▷ {before_LC}) = v_inside(r0 ↦ cz0)
inv3 : dom(v_position ▷ {inside_LC}) = v_inside(cz0 ↦ cz1)
inv4 : dom(v_position ▷ {after_LC}) = v_inside(cz1 ↦ r1)
inv5 : ∀v·v_position(v) = away_LC ⇒ (∀x·x ∈ ran(v_inside) ⇒ v ∉ x)
```

4.7 Formal Specification of the Machine M4

This level introduces a new variable called *v_number* defined by the following invariant: $v\_number \in dom(v\_position \triangleright \{before\_LC\}) \rightarrowtail 1..card(dom(v\_position \triangleright \{before\_LC\}))$. This variable assigns a unique number to each vehicle as it enters the road on the side before the crossing zone. The first vehicle to enter is assigned the number one, and the last one is assigned the total number of vehicles. Thereby, the gateway has more control over the vehicles and knows exactly which vehicle should cross the railway. Then, each vehicle gets its *v_number* after performing a connection with the gateway. After that, the *v_number* is updated after the vehicle passes through the LC zone.

Two events are refined at this level: *enter_road* and *enter_road_LC*. The guard component of the first event is reinforced by three guards. Let n be the number of vehicles in the $(r0 \mapsto cz0)$ path, then n should be less than the threshold *max_cars_before_LC*: $n < max\_cars\_before\_LC$. If there are no vehicles inside the $(r0 \mapsto cz0)$ path then, n gets the value zero: $v\_number = \varnothing \Rightarrow n = 0$, otherwise n gets the number of the last entered vehicle: $v\_number \neq \varnothing \Rightarrow max(ran(v\_number)) = n$. In the action component the entered vehicle gets a new number which is $n+1$: $v\_number := v\_number \cup \{vehicule \mapsto n+1\}$.

The second event *enter_road_LC* is reinforced by a new guard, which allows only the vehicle *vehicule* that has number one (i.e., the first in front of the crossing zone) to cross the railway: $v\_number(vehicule) = 1$. In the action component of this event, we update the whole number of vehicles inside the $(r0 \mapsto cz0)$ path: $v\_number := \{x, y \cdot x \in dom(v\_number) \wedge v\_number(x) > 1 \wedge v\_number(x) = y | x \mapsto (y - 1)\}$

4.8 Overview of Proof Obligations

In Table 3, we give an overview of the proof statistics for the development of the railway LC system using the RODIN platform. These statistics are a measure of the development complexity. Some Proof Obligations (POs) are produced and automatically discharged by RODIN while others are interactively proved. There are 235 POs generated by the RODIN platform. 116 POs (49%) are automatically discharged, while the others (119 POs = 51%) which are more complex and require the interaction with the provers.

Table 3. Proof statistics

Models	Total POs	Automatic POs (%)	Interactive POs (%)
Contexts	0	0	0
Machine M0	39	11 (28%)	28 (72%)
Machine M1	59	38 (64%)	21 (36%)
Machine M2	68	40 (59%)	28 (41%)
Machine M3	50	21 (42%)	29 (58%)
Machine M4	19	6 (32%)	13 (68%)
Total	235	116 (49%)	119 (51%)

5 Related Work

Several works have been proposed to verify the correctness of railway LC control systems. Most of the reviewed approaches have used the model checking-method [15], which is easy to understand and relies on automated techniques that can perform a faster evaluation. For instance, the authors of [14] defined a new automatic protection system architecture that avoids two particular scenarios, which have been identified as the reasons for many LC accidents. The first scenario is the short opening duration between successive closure cycles related to trains passing in opposite directions. The second scenario is the long closure duration correlated with slow trains. Therefore, the proposed architecture consists in adding an anticipation sensor and a speed sensor prior to the usual train detection sensor on the arrival side. This architecture has been validated using formal notations based on timed automata [4] for the specification phase and the model-checking technique for the verification process. Nevertheless, adopting model checking-based verification has some limitations. Indeed, when the state space is too large, it suffers from the state explosion problem.

Moreover, many research studies [10,16,18] focused on hiding formal methods-related details by automating model transformations for railway systems engineering. Therefore, they can achieve a formal verification result without learning the necessary mathematical background. In [10], Kraibi et al. introduced an approach combining the UML (Unified Modeling Language) [8] and Event-B formal method. In fact, the authors used UML to model the system behavior from an informal specification. Then, the UML model is translated into Event-B model, and proceeded with the formal verification and validation of safety properties using formal proof techniques. The proposed approach is illustrated through a case study of a railway signaling system.

Authors in [13] introduced a formal model-based methodology that assists the building of a safe electronic urban railway control system. This methodology consists in selecting and integrating an appropriate high-level semi-formal and low-level formal description forms and tools into a toolchain that fits the railway field. Moreover, it ensures the transformation from semi-formal to formal models. Besides, it takes into consideration the specificities of the studied domain and the best-practice engineering systems. In fact, the proposed methodology has been illustrated via a case study of a tram-road LC protection system which has a simple architecture and a low number of elements.

The contribution of Rehman et al. [17] presents a graphical model of the railway gate control system based on the UML. Then, the authors transferred the UML sequence diagram into the Deterministic Finite Automata (DFA) realizing the functions of the system. Additionally, the automata-based model is transformed into a formal model using the VDM-SL formal language [11]. This model is verified and checked through the VDM-SL toolbox[1].

To the best of our knowledge, only few studies have adopted the theorem proving-based verification [7] which adopts hard-proof mechanisms that require the user's interaction. Nevertheless, it ensures a powerful correctness method and can deal with complex formalisms. In [3], the authors formalised a generic hybrid railway signalling model using the Event-B formal method and communication modeling patterns. This model introduces railway signalling sub-systems that can compute and communicate safe travelling distances to the rolling stock. It can be extended by refinement to capture a particular signalling configuration.

In this work, we introduce a railway LC system which is based on vehicle to infrastructure communication in order to enhance security during LC. The correctness of the proposed system has been verified using the Event-B formal method and the refinement technique.

---

[1] https://www.overturetool.org/download/examples/VDMSL/.

6 Conclusion

In this research, we have attempted to suggest a new railway LC system that prevents the main risky situations. The proposed system is specified by a formal model using the Event-B method. In fact, we are based on a stepwise refinement strategy to build a correct solution. Then, the correctness of our model is checked by discharging all the proof obligations.

One of the future work directions is to address the inter-vehicle communications which can meet stringent safety application. Moreover, we aim to enhance our work by verifying the correctness of temporal properties, such as liveness properties which can not be checked using invariants.

References

1. Abrial, J.R.: Modeling in Event-B: System and Software Engineering. Cambridge University Press, Cambridge (2010)
2. Abrial, J.R., Butler, M., Hallerstede, S., Hoang, T., Mehta, F., Voisin, L.: Rodin: an open toolset for modelling and reasoning in event-b. Int. J. Softw. Tools Technol. Transf. (STTT) 12(6), 447–466 (2010)
3. Aït-Ameur, Y., Bogomolov, S., Dupont, G., Iliasov, A., Romanovsky, A., Stankaitis, P.: A refinement-based formal development of cyber-physical railway signalling systems. Form. Asp. Comput. 35(1), 1, 3 (2023). https://doi.org/10.1145/3524052
4. Alur, R.: Timed automata. In: Halbwachs, N., Peled, D. (eds.) CAV 1999. LNCS, vol. 1633, pp. 8–22. Springer, Heidelberg (1999). https://doi.org/10.1007/3-540-48683-6_3
5. Badeau, F., Amelot, A.: Using B as a high level programming language in an industrial project: roissy VAL. In: Treharne, H., King, S., Henson, M., Schneider, S. (eds.) ZB 2005. LNCS, vol. 3455, pp. 334–354. Springer, Heidelberg (2005). https://doi.org/10.1007/11415787_20
6. Behm, P., Benoit, P., Faivre, A., Meynadier, J.-M.: Météor: a successful application of b in a large project. In: Wing, J.M., Woodcock, J., Davies, J. (eds.) FM 1999. LNCS, vol. 1708, pp. 369–387. Springer, Heidelberg (1999). https://doi.org/10.1007/3-540-48119-2_22
7. Green, C.: Application of theorem proving to problem solving. In: Readings in Artificial Intelligence, pp. 202–222. Elsevier (1981)
8. Jacobson, I., Booch, G., Rumbaugh, J.: The unified modeling language. University Video Communications (1996)
9. Kourie, D.G., Watson, B.W.: The Correctness-by-Construction Approach to Programming. Springer, Berlin, Heidelberg (2012). https://doi.org/10.1007/978-3-642-27919-5
10. Kraibi, K., Ayed, R.B., Collart-Dutilleul, S., Bon, P., Petit, D.: Analysis and formal modeling of systems behavior using UML/event-B. J. Commun. 14(10), 980–986 (2019)
11. Larsen, P.G., Pawlowski, W.: The formal semantics of ISO VDM-SL. Comput. Stand. Interfaces 17(5–6), 585–601 (1995)
12. Liu, B., Ghazel, M., Toguyéni, A.: Model-based diagnosis of multi-track level crossing plants. IEEE Trans. Intell. Transp. Syst. 17(2), 546–556 (2015)

13. Lukács, G., Bartha, T.: Formal modeling and verification of the functionality of electronic urban railway control systems through a case study. Urban Rail Transit **8**(3), 217–245 (2022)
14. Mekki, A., Ghazel, M., Toguyeni, A.: Validation of a new functional design of automatic protection systems at level crossings with model-checking techniques. IEEE Trans. Intell. Transp. Syst. (T-ITS) **13**(2), 714–723 (2012)
15. Müller-Olm, M., Schmidt, D., Steffen, B.: Model-checking. In: Cortesi, A., Filé, G. (eds.) SAS 1999. LNCS, vol. 1694, pp. 330–354. Springer, Heidelberg (1999). https://doi.org/10.1007/3-540-48294-6_22
16. Rao, L., Liu, S., Peng, H.: An integrated formal method combining labeled transition system and event-B for system model refinement. IEEE Access **10**, 13089–13102 (2022)
17. Rehman, A., Latif, S., Zafar, N.A.: Automata based railway gate control system at level crossing. In: International Conference on Communication Technologies (ComTech), pp. 30–35. IEEE (2019)
18. Weidmann, N., Salunkhe, S., Anjorin, A., Yigitbas, E., Engels, G.: Automating model transformations for railway systems engineering. J. Object Technol. (JOT) **20**(3), 10–1 (2021)

Author Index

Printed in the United States
by Baker & Taylor Publisher Services